KEYS
TO THE
KINGDOM

FOUND IN THE PARABLES

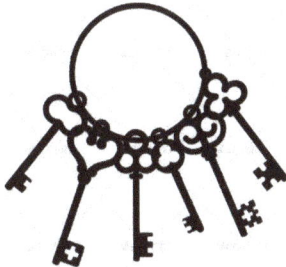

BY

TOM MCMANUS

Cover photo by Deeb G. Dides, http://deebdides.wix.com/webpage

Published by:

Kingdom Come Books
www.thepublishedword.com

ISBN: 978-1-950398-06-5

Printed in the U.S., the U.K., Australia, and the U.A.E,
For Worldwide Distribution

Dedication

To my God who is King of kings and Lord of lords. Your love is everlasting. It is boundless in its height, depth, width and breath. I am humbled to speak of who You are, for it is a mere speck of Your awesome holy majesty. May You be glorified in all that is written here.

ACKNOWLEDGEMENTS

One day I just happened to stumble across a book written by Dale Sides entitled *The 1,000 Year Reign of Jesus Christ on the Earth.*[1] That book provided insights that would put many pieces of the puzzle together for me. I so appreciate the forerunner work Dale does and his love of our King.

I want to thank my wonderful wife and dear friend, Janie, the mother of our three fabulous children and grandmother of our eight buzzing grandchildren. We have been on mountains and been through valleys and have eaten sumptuous locust and wild honey in the desert with joy together.

---

1. Sides, Dale, *The 1,000 Year Reign of Jesus Christ on the Earth* (Bedford, VA: Liberating Publications, 2006)

Contents

Introduction..7

1. The Fear of the Lord...11
2. Seeing Differently 18
3. An End-Time Timeline 25
4. The Coming Millennial Kingdom 43
5. What Is the Kingdom of Heaven? 48
6. How Will One Be Judged At the Judgment Seat of Christ?.............54
7. What Happens to Those Who Miss the Kingdom of Heaven? 63
8. The Two Inheritances...75
9. The First Resurrection..83
10. The Parable of the Ten Virgins.....................................86
11. The Parable of the Dragnet...92
12. The Parable of the Wheat and Tares 95
13. From the Resurrection to the Judgment Seat 99
14. The Judgment Seat of Christ 115
15. The Parable of the Talents..119
16. The Parable of the Unforgiving Servant.......................124
17. The Parable of the Wedding Feast................................127
18. The Son of Man Judges the Nations.............................132
19. How the Fall Feasts Could be Fulfilled 141
20. The Second Death 147
21. This Sounds Like Purgatory..157
22. A Letter to the Laodicean Church 175
23. Divorce and Remarriage...184
24. Being Ready for Tribulation..195
25. The Parable of the Sower 204
26. So, What Now? 208
    Author Contact Page 218

*And I will give you **the keys of the kingdom of heaven,** and whatever you bind on earth will be bound in heaven, and whatever you loose on earth will be loosed in heaven.*

Matthew 16:19

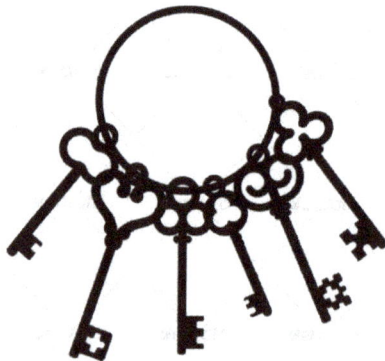

INTRODUCTION

Matthew 13:10-13

*And the disciples came and said to Him, "Why do You speak to them in parables?" He answered and said to them, "Because **it has been given to you to know the mysteries of the kingdom of heaven**, but to them it has not been given. For whoever has, to him more will be given, and he will have abundance; but whoever does not have, even what he has will be taken away from him. **Therefore I speak to them in parables, because seeing they do not see, and hearing they do not hear, nor do they understand**."*

Interestingly, after Jesus said, *"It has been given to you to know the mysteries of the kingdom of heaven,"* the very first parable He told began with the words *"The kingdom of heaven **is like**,"* not the Kingdom of Heaven **is**. The parables are **keys** to solving this mystery, and that is what we will venture to do in this book—solve the mystery.

We don't understand the true meaning of the parables because we have eyes that do not see and ears that do not hear. Many, including the handpicked disciples of Jesus, were left scratching their heads, not having a clue as to what He was actually saying.

Mark 4:13

And He said to them, "Do you not understand this parable? How then will you understand all the parables?"

7

The disciples pursued Jesus for the interpretation of what the parables meant.

Mark 4:33-34

And with many such parables He spoke the word to them as they were able to hear it. But without a parable He did not speak to them. And when they were alone, He explained all things to His disciples.

If you are like me, you like doctrine to be black and white. There's the scripture. I believe it, and that settles it. Yet, the Lord hides truths in parables and enjoys it when we pursue Him to receive more understanding of them.

Proverbs 25:2, NASB

It is the glory of God to conceal a matter,
But the glory of kings is to search out a matter.

Jesus told the Church of Laodicea: *"Anoint your eyes with eye salve, that you may see."* We will only anoint our eyes when we have convinced ourselves that there are some things we just don't see well enough yet.

Let me show you a picture that many of you may have seen already. I was first introduced to this picture by one of my high school teachers. He split our class into two groups and sent one group outside the classroom into the hallway.

He then outlined the shape of a beautiful young woman to the group in the classroom. The groups traded places, and when the new group came in, he outlined the shape of an old hag in the picture. (Here's a hint about this picture: The chin of the young woman is the nose of the hag, and the necklace of the young woman is the mouth of the hag. See if you can see both perspectives.)

The two groups were brought together, asked to be seated and questioned as to what they saw. One group said a beautiful young woman, while the other group responded quickly with a laugh that it was an old hag. This went back and forth until there was feisty shouting. It wasn't until the teacher allowed the students to come forward and outline the eyes, nose and chin of their prospective woman that they understood what the other was talking about. Each group had no question as to what they saw. It was as plain as night and day, and yet, as they allowed themselves to listen to what the others were saying, they began to see the image differently. Those who were the most steadfast in their viewpoint were the last to see what was there.

As I speak about the parables in the coming pages, it will be as though I am showing you a third woman in the picture, a totally different women you don't yet see. I'm taking the time to talk about seeing differently because I know it is hard for me to process new information that doesn't fit into my established theology. I, too, am guarded and do not want to be tossed to and fro by every new wind of doctrine.

My appeal would be this: in order for you to understand what I am trying to say, please follow my pointer (so to speak) until ... we are able to see the picture together. It's very difficult to process ideas that disrupt our established belief structure. Sometimes we can viscerally feel a shaking in our inner man. If you are like me, it is in those times that we can flip a switch in our brain which is the "No" button. This provides temporary relief from having our understanding challenged. When we switch to "No," we are unable to hear much of anything but that "No." I'm embarrassed at how often I have done this very thing. I think that is what the Scriptures talk about when they say *"ears that do not hear."* I am convinced that you will have insights that I haven't seen, and I pray that I will hear your comments without fearing that all my great premises will fall like a stack of Jenga blocks ... if what you say is true.

What I don't want to do is just go through the exercise of looking at a new eschatology for something else we can differ on. What I hope we will find is that Jesus spoke some very direct and stern warnings to His people, warnings that need to be understood, and if we miss them, we will suffer the consequences of having eyes that do not see. If we understand the fear of the Lord and long for the sanctifying work of the Spirit, we will be ready for Christ's coming. The Lord desires that each will receive the fullness of the inheritance that He has for all who believe.

Tom McManus
North Carolina

CHAPTER 1

THE FEAR OF THE LORD

The purpose of these writings is to warn the Body of Christ of impending judgment that we will face if we do not repent. You may say that this sounds as exciting as a trip to the dentist, but just like going to the dentist, your efforts in reading through this may prevent future pain.

If you ask most believers, "Why should you fear the Lord?" many would answer, "I don't know." Most of us think very little about judgment and assume that we will go straight to Heaven, lie upon a cloud and play a musical instrument forever.

Others would answer that they fear going to Hell. When asked what they must do to be confident they will *not* go to Hell, many give answers that are vague and lacking surety. Knowing what it is that we should fear and what to do to stand confidently before the Lord is the wisdom we need.

Proverbs 14:27

> *The fear of the LORD is a fountain of life,*
> *To turn one away from the snares of death.*

Now, having the fear of the Lord is different from being afraid of God, although they may seem the same. The fear of the Lord is always good, but being afraid of God is a sin. If you are afraid of God, you might think He is mean, unjust, uncaring or unforgiving. These things are contrary to the true character of God and defame Him.

Some would say that they have nothing to fear, for God has forgiven them all their sins and Christ sees them as perfect. Certainly, God will limitlessly forgive those who repent and ask for His forgiveness, but what about those sins that believers fail to repent of? When Christ spoke to the seven churches in Revelation 2 and 3, He didn't see them as perfect; He saw them exactly as they were, with all their weaknesses and strengths. He called them to repent and listed a variety of consequences they would suffer if they failed to do so. So, Jesus sees the good and bad in us, and here is what He will do when He judges us.

2 Corinthians 5:10

For we must all appear before the judgment seat of Christ, that each one may receive the things done in the body, according to what he has done, whether good or bad.

All believers will stand before the Judgment Seat of Christ; there will be no unbelievers present. You may or may not know that the Judgment Seat of Christ is different from the Great White Throne Judgment, but we will go over that distinction further on. Unfortunately, you have probably never heard a sermon about the Judgment Seat of Christ, and yet it is, by far, the most important event of your life and one that you are quickly approaching.

We will all be judged according to what we have done, whether good or bad. The "bad" will be sin that has not been repented of, for all sin that has been repented of is forgiven and forgotten (see 1 John 1:9). So, what are some of the "bad" things we could be found doing? Here's an example:

Matthew 6:15

But if you do not forgive men their trespasses, neither will your Father forgive your trespasses.

Would you not need to pay a penalty for those sins that have not been forgiven?

Matthew 7:2

For with what judgment you judge, you will be judged; and with the measure you use, it will be measured back to you. If you judge someone harshly you will be judged harshly.

James 2:13

For judgment is without mercy to the one who has shown no mercy. Mercy triumphs over judgment.

If you show no mercy, you will not receive mercy yourself.

You may be quite familiar with these scriptures. They were given as stern warnings to believers (not unbelievers), so that we would not suffer the specified repercussions. So, what does it mean to not have your sins forgiven? What does it mean to be judged harshly? What does it mean not to receive mercy? And what are the consequences we should fear if we are found in these sins?

To answer, we'll be looking at Matthew 5, where Jesus delineated the difference between the Old Covenant and the New. He also clearly clarified His new standard for what He considered sin and what the punishment for that sin would be.

Matthew 5:21-22 and 27-30

You have heard that it was said to those of old, "You shall not murder, and whoever murders will be in danger of the judgment." But I say to you that whoever is angry with his brother without a cause shall be in danger of the judgment. And whoever says to his brother, "Raca!" shall be in danger of the council. But whoever says, "You fool!" shall be in danger of **hell fire.**

You have heard that it was said to those of old, "You shall not commit adultery." But I say to you that whoever looks at a woman to lust for her has already committed adultery with her in his heart. If your right eye causes you to sin, pluck it out and cast it from you; for it is more profitable for you that one of your members perish, than for your whole body to be cast into **hell**. *And if your right hand causes you to sin, cut it off and cast it from you; for it is more profitable for you that one of your members perish, than for your whole body to be cast into* **hell**.

Jesus began by saying, *"You have heard that it was said to those of old, 'You shall not murder.'"* This is the Old Covenant, the Ten Commandments. He then said, "But I say to you, 'If you call someone a fool, you could be subject to Hell fire.'" These are the New Covenant guidelines and the punishment for disobedience. I'm not making this up. This is Christ's new mandate for those who believe.

Then He did it again. He said, *"You have heard it said, 'You shall not commit adultery.' "* This is from the Old Covenant, the Ten Commandments. Then Jesus said, *"But I say to you that whoever looks at a woman to lust for her has already committed adultery with her in his heart."* This is again the New Covenant guideline.

But wait a minute! I thought the New Covenant was supposed to be easier than keeping the Law. It is a lot easier not to kill someone or not to have illicit sexual relations with someone than it is not to judge someone or not to lust after a woman in one's heart (especially at a beach on a summer day). Jesus was saying, "I'm not interested in whether or not you appear to be a religious person on the outside; I will be judging your heart. I will be judging whether you have murder or lust hidden there."

Wow! A few could obey the Law, but it is beyond everyone to fulfill these new higher standards. Jesus knew this, and His solution was quite easy: repent and be forgiven. And what if you sin again? Repent again and be forgiven, and repeat the process as often as needed. The sanctification of the heart cannot be done in our own strength. It requires a constant fellowship with Christ. As the Spirit leads us, we repent and are washed and cleansed from all iniquity.

Jesus declared this New Covenant in the midst of a religious system full of religious men who rejected God but worked feverishly on their outward appearance. He knew that His disciples might not fully understand what He was saying, so He emphasized the point:

> *If your right eye causes you to sin, pluck it out and cast it from you; for it is more profitable for you that one of your members perish, than for your whole body to be cast into* **hell.** *And if your right hand causes you to sin, cut it off and cast it from you; for it is more profitable for you that one of your members perish, than for your whole body to be cast into* **hell.**

These words mean something, and they are not to be ignored or minimized. This was (and is) a word to believers, the righteous ones who were (and are) moving into the New Covenant. Obviously Jesus was not promoting self-mutilation. He was saying, in no uncertain terms, that if your eye causes you to lust, it would be better for you to pluck it out than to go to Hell. If your computer is causing you to be entangled with internet porn and you can't stop, then throw it out the window. It's better that you lose a computer than suffer Hell fire. If your right hand causes you to point an accusatory finger or hurt someone, then it is better to cut it off. Hell is so bad that it cannot be compared to the temporary pain of plucking out your eye or cutting off your arm.

Christ spoke very clearly and directly as to how He will one day judge believers, but these words have been ignored or displaced with man's ideas on the topic. When we take a look at how He will judge us, we will understand the fear of the Lord. Remember, the fear of the Lord is a good thing.

Job 28:28

And to man He said,
"Behold, the fear of the LORD, that is wisdom,
And to depart from evil is understanding."

So how does the Body of Christ view Hell as it relates to believers? Many teach that there will be no punishment for the believer—only a loss of rewards. Thus, the warnings from Jesus land on deaf ears. There are others who believe that if one persists in sin, he can lose his salvation and end up in the Hell (which he believes is the Lake of Fire). Both of these understandings fall short. We'll be looking beyond the Calvinistic/Armenian paradigm to find the real answers.

So what is hell? We will see that there are three words that are translated as Hell—*gehenna, tartarus* and *hades.* We will see that each of these is distinct from the others. Just about everyone who would use Hell in a sentence would understand it as a fiery place of judgment where one experiences the wrath of God forever. Revelation 20 describes the Lake of Fire and Brimstone as the place where the devil (Satan), the False Prophet and the Beast are cast, along with those whose names are not written in the Book of Life. Further on, I want to prove to you that **Hell is not the Lake of Fire.** This alone is worth the price of the book.

It is essential to understand what Hell (*Gehenna*) is, since Jesus warned His disciples numerous times of the consequences of Hell (*Gehenna*) for being carnal. He never warned the Gentiles concerning

Hell (*Gehenna*). Jesus was not saying that a believer would experience eternal wrath in the Lake of Fire if they were found in lust or judging others. So, what is the fiery consequence that He is speaking of?

CHAPTER 2

SEEING DIFFERENTLY

I want to give you an interpretation of a parable that you probably haven't heard before. It will reveal what Hell (*Gehenna*) is. First, let's read the Parable of the Unforgiving Servant:

Matthew 18:21-35

*Then Peter came to Him and said, "Lord, how often shall my brother sin against me, and I forgive him? Up to seven times?" Jesus said to him, "I do not say to you, up to seven times, but up to seventy times seven. Therefore **the kingdom of heaven is like** a certain king who wanted to settle accounts with his servants. And when he had begun to settle accounts, one was brought to him who owed him ten thousand talents. But as he was not able to pay, his master commanded that he be sold, with his wife and children and all that he had, and that payment be made. The servant therefore fell down before him, saying, "Master, have patience with me, and I will pay you all." Then the master of that servant was moved with compassion, released him, and forgave him the debt.*

But that servant went out and found one of his fellow servants who owed him a hundred denarii; and he laid hands on him and took him by the throat, saying, "Pay me what you owe!" So his fellow servant fell down at his feet and begged him, saying, "Have patience with me, and I will pay you all." And he would not, but went and threw him into prison till he should pay the debt. So when his fellow servants saw what had been done, they were very grieved, and came and told their master all that had been done. Then his master, after he had called him, said to him, "You wicked servant! I forgave you all that debt because you begged me. Should you not also have had compassion on your fellow servant, just as I had pity on you?" And his master was angry, and delivered him to the torturers until he should pay all that was due to him. So My heavenly Father also will do to you if each of you, from his heart, does not forgive his brother his trespasses.

Here we have a master who wanted to settle accounts with his servants. One servant owed the master 10,000 talents (150,000 years of salary), which he was not able to pay. *"The master commanded that he be sold, with his wife and children and all that he had, and that payment be made."* The servant and his family were to be sold as slaves for life to pay the debt. Before this judgment could be executed, however, the servant fell down before his master (also translated as *worshiped* the master). He said, *"Master, have patience with me, and I will pay you all."* As a result, *"Then the master of that servant was moved with compassion, released him, and forgave him the debt."*

Who does this servant with the great debt represent? Think about it. Who do you know who has been forgiven much? All of us owe a debt (of sin) that is impossible to pay by any natural means, and therefore, this is the judgment we all face without Christ's redemption. When unbelievers understand the consequences of their debt, they cry out to God for mercy. The master, who represents God Himself, heard the cry of the debtor, had compassion on him and forgave him his debt. This shows that the servant who asks for forgiveness receives salvation with the cancellation of his debt of sin.

Act 3:19

Repent therefore and be converted, that your sins may be blotted out, so that times of refreshing may come from the presence of the Lord.

Colossians 2:14, NIV

Having canceled the charge of our legal indebtedness, which stood against us and condemned us; he has taken it away, nailing it to the cross.

The man who was forgiven much represents each of us who have believed in Christ and been born again.

Then, however, that believer went out and threw someone in jail who owed him a small debt. The result was that the master called the one who had been forgiven much to stand before him and held him accountable for what he had done. This speaks of the Judgment Seat of Christ, the place where all believers will be judged for all things done and all things left undone.

Romans 14:10-12

*But why do you judge your brother? Or why do you show contempt for your brother? For we shall all stand before **the judgment seat of Christ**. For it is written:*

"As I live, says the LORD,
Every knee shall bow to Me,
And every tongue shall confess to God."

So then each of us shall give account of himself to God.

The master was extremely angry and told the tormenters (jailers) to take the man away until his debt could be paid. Notice that the man was not to be confined to jail forever—only until his debt was paid. Then he would be released. This punishment, then, is distinct from the eternal wrath of the Lake of Fire reserved for unbelievers, in that it has an end. That end comes when the debt is paid.

Now, look at the very next verse and remember that Jesus was telling the story:

So My heavenly Father also will do to you if each of you, from his heart, does not forgive his brother his trespasses (verse 35).

Who was Jesus talking to here when He had said, *"So My heavenly Father also will do to you?"* It was Peter who asked, *"Lord, how often shall my brother sin against me, and I forgive him? Up to seven times?"* And it was in response to Peter's question that the Lord told this Parable of the Unforgiving Servant. So, the Lord was speaking directly to the disciples here, not to the unbelieving. This, then, is how Jesus said His Father would judge believers who fail to forgive from the **heart**. This is about more than just lip service. Jesus was affirming that He would be judging the hearts of men.

Have you ever heard a sermon that informed believers that they would be imprisoned after the Judgment Seat of Christ until their debt was paid if they had unforgiveness in their heart? Our understanding of God's judgment on unforgiveness cannot be modified or watered down because we think it is too harsh or doesn't fit into our theology.

Our response should be clear. We must forgive in the same way we have been forgiven. Is this important? We can test our interpretation of this parable and see if it aligns with other scriptures.

Matthew 6:14-15

For if you forgive men their trespasses, your heavenly Father will also forgive you. But if you do not forgive men their trespasses, neither will your Father forgive your trespasses.

21

Do you understand this scripture more clearly now, or are you beginning to? The following scriptures are spoken to believers, and the judgment that is spoken of will happen at the Judgment Seat of Christ:

Matthew 7:2

For with what judgment you judge, you will be judged; and with the measure you use, it will be measured back to you.

James 2:13

For judgment is without mercy to the one who has shown no mercy. Mercy triumphs over judgment.

We have all been offended by others and, generally speaking, can recognize whether we have truly forgiven someone or not. All someone has to do is walk in the door, and our heart will tell us how we feel in this regard. We are required to give our bitterness, anger and resentments to Christ and allow love for our enemies to reign in our hearts. This is an impossible task for the carnal man, but as we submit our hearts to Christ through confession and repentance by faith, we are transformed by the Spirit of God. We can be confident that Christ will cleanse us from all iniquity as we confess our sins to Him.

You may say that all your sins—past, present and future—are forgiven at the cross and, although this sounds good, is it true if one has unforgiveness in their heart? Jesus was exhorting His people to repent and be ready at His coming or suffer judgment. Remember, the servant received the elimination of all his debt, but, because of his judgment on someone who owed *him* money, he was judged in the same way, and his debt was reinstated.

We saw earlier in the book that Jesus knew that the parables would not be understood by many. He knew that man's traditions and doctrines would negate what He would say in the parables.

Matthew 13:15

For the hearts of this people have grown dull.
Their ears are hard of hearing,
And their eyes they have closed,
Lest they should see with their eyes and hear with their ears,
Lest they should understand with their hearts and turn,
So that I should heal them.

If they had eyes to see and ears to hear, they would understand and repent, and then He would forgive them and restore them. We will see that the parables are like prophetic declarations to warn God's people of what will happen at the end of this age.

Here are corresponding verses that line up precisely with the Parable of the Unforgiving Servant.

Matthew 5:23-26

*Therefore if you bring your gift to the altar, and there remember that your brother has something against you, leave your gift there before the altar, and go your way. First be reconciled to your brother, and then come and offer your gift. Agree with your adversary quickly, while you are on the way with him, lest your adversary deliver you to the judge, **the judge hand you over to the officer, and you be thrown into prison.** Assuredly, I say to you, **you will by no means get out of there till you have paid the last penny**.*

Again, Jesus was not talking to an unbeliever, but to a believer, one who was bringing his gift to the altar. He said that if you remember that someone has something against you, then leave the gift before the altar and be reconciled, and then come and offer your gift. Understand that if you have unforgiveness in your heart, Jesus is not interested in your gifts or Christian service. They are actually detestable to Him. This is not to be ignored. One must reconcile quickly, for judgment will be made swiftly, and the cost will be exacting.

We see here again that Jesus quite clearly stated that a believer can be thrown into prison. This, again, is not to be confused with the eternal punishment of the Lake of Fire, since this prison term has an end, and that end comes when the debt is paid off. Then that person is released. I would suggest that even though a believer can suffer a temporary punishment, they will receive eternal life, which is an inheritance that is given them through faith and cannot be lost.

Although the interpretation of these scriptures might bear witness with your spirit, you may have a hard time figuring out how this could fit into your present understanding. I will endeavor to show you how these events will work together in the coming chapters. Remember, I'm drawing a picture here, and I'm not done yet.

I want to make a quick note here that this book is not associated with the Catholic doctrine of purgatory, although you may find some similarities. In fact, we will discuss in more detail the stark distinctions between this study and purgatory. If you have disdain for anything remotely sounding like purgatory, I fully understand, especially considering the aberrant use of indulgences by Catholic priests to atone for punishment in purgatory. I would suggest that the doctrine of purgatory and the Reformers' reaction against it has been the chief cause for our current lack of understanding concerning Hell (*Gehenna*), the Judgment Seat of Christ and the parables. You will find that our discussion will not take either a Catholic or Protestant viewpoint, but something that is uniquely different.

If you need to, you can skip over to Chapter 20 "This Sounds Like Purgatory" to see the distinctions we make. With that said, I hope we can look afresh at the Scriptures and see what Jesus has to say about Hell and judgment.

CHAPTER 3

AN END-TIME TIMELINE

I know that this interpretation of the Parable of the Unforgiving Servant may be new to many, including seasoned believers. We know that the words of Jesus have meaning and should not be disregarded. Yet, for many, it is difficult to understand how and when this temporary punishment of Hell (*Gehenna*) will take place. In order for me to explain how a believer could experience Hell (*Gehenna*) and yet receive an inheritance of eternal life, it is essential to look at end-time events.

We will go through Revelation 19:11–21:8 to get an overview of what will happen at the end of this age and on into the ages to come. We will see the Battle of Armageddon, the establishment of Jesus' thousand-year reign on the earth, the different judgment seats and the New Heaven and New Earth. We will go through all of this so that we might understand how what is spoken in the parables can happen within the end-time sequence of events.

The coming of Jesus will mark the end of this age and the beginning of the next.

Revelation 19:11-19

Now I saw heaven opened, and behold, a white horse. And He who sat on him was called Faithful and True, and in righteousness He judges and makes war. His eyes were like a flame of fire, and on His head were many crowns. He had a name written that no one knew except Himself. He was clothed with a robe dipped in blood, and His name is called The Word of God. And the armies in heaven, clothed in fine linen, white and clean, followed Him on white horses. **Now out of His mouth goes a sharp sword, that with it He should strike the nations. And He Himself will rule them with a rod of iron. He Himself treads the winepress of the fierceness and wrath of Almighty God.** *And He has on His robe and on His thigh a name written:*

KING OF KINGS AND
LORD OF LORDS.

Then I saw an angel standing in the sun; and he cried with a loud voice, saying to all the birds that fly in the midst of heaven, "Come and gather together for the supper of the great God, that you may eat the flesh of kings, the flesh of captains, the flesh of mighty men, the flesh of horses and of those who sit on them, and the flesh of all people, free and slave, both small and great."

And I saw the beast, the kings of the earth, and their armies, gathered together to make war against Him who sat on the horse and against His army.

The illustrations that follow are on a timeline which moves from left to right, past to future. The horizontal line denotes the Earth. Above the Earth represents the heavens, and below represents the placement for Death, Hades and the Lake of Fire. Scriptures will be highlighted in each illustration.

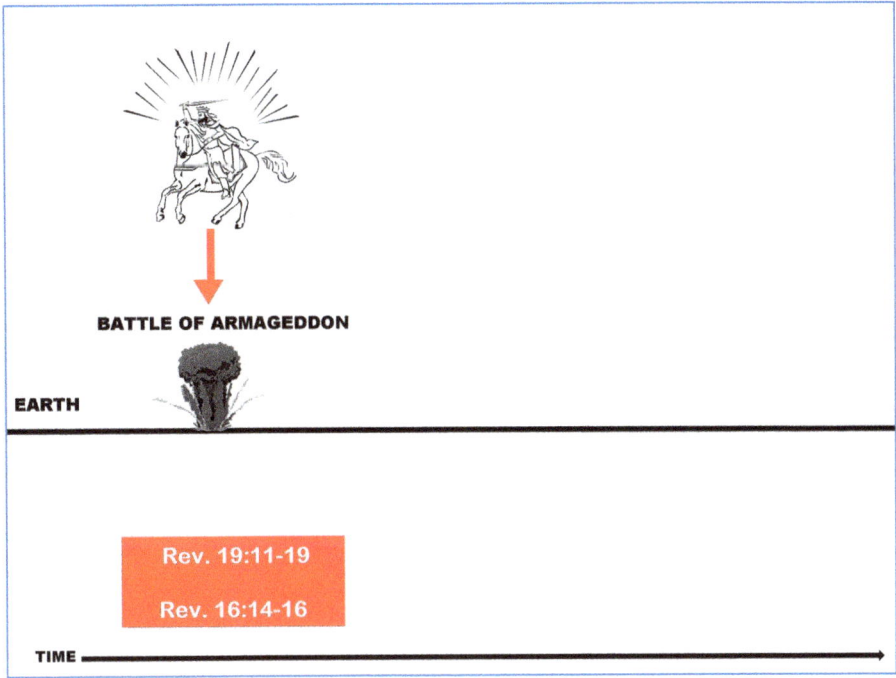

BATTLE OF ARMAGEDDON

EARTH

Rev. 19:11-19

Rev. 16:14-16

TIME

Revelation 19:20-21

Then the beast was captured, and with him the false prophet who worked signs in his presence, by which he deceived those who received the mark of the beast and those who worshiped his image. These two were cast alive into the lake of fire burning with brimstone. And the rest were killed with the sword which proceeded from the mouth of Him who sat on the horse. And all the birds were filled with their flesh.

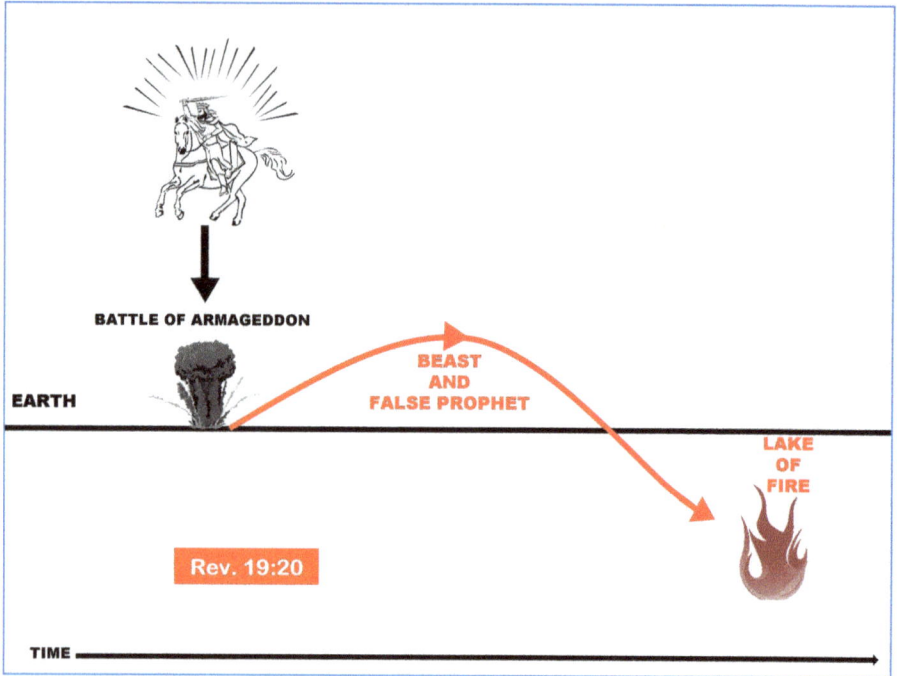

This chart shows the Beast and False Prophet thrown alive into the Lake of Fire. Let's continue:

Revelation 20:1-3

Then I saw an angel coming down from heaven, having the key to the bottomless pit and a great chain in his hand. He laid hold of the dragon, that serpent of old, who is the Devil and Satan, and bound him for a thousand years; and he cast him into the bottomless pit, and shut him up, and set a seal on him, so that he should deceive the nations no more till the thousand years were finished. But after these things he must be released for a little while.

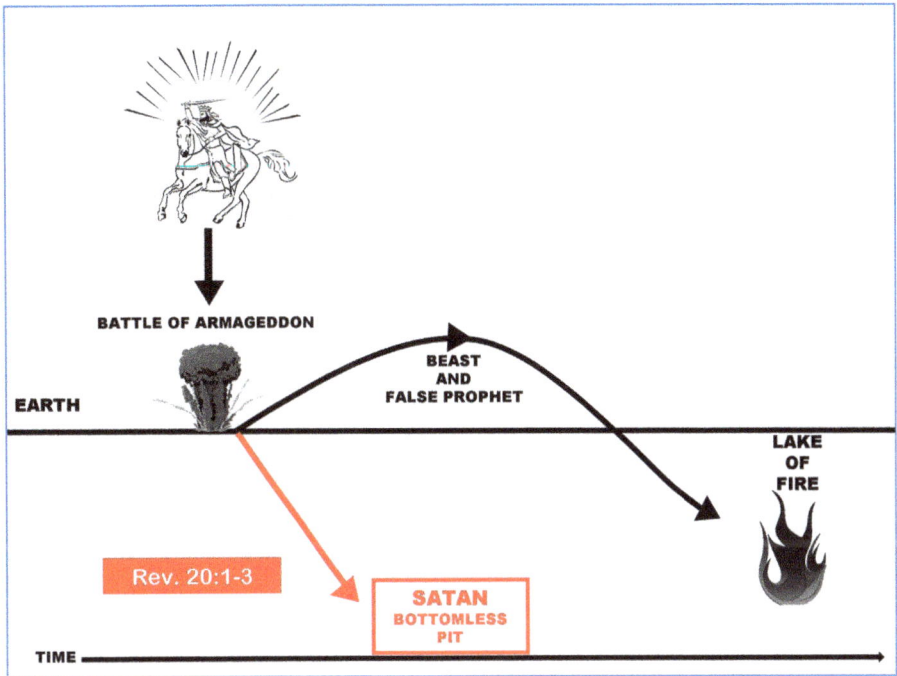

This chart shows that Satan is bound in the Bottomless Pit for a thousand years.

Revelation 20:4-6

And I saw thrones, and they sat on them, and judgment was committed to them. Then I saw the souls of those who had been beheaded for their witness to Jesus and for the word of God, who had not worshiped the beast or his image, and had not received his mark on their foreheads or on their hands. And they lived and reigned with Christ for a thousand years. But the rest of the dead did not live again until the thousand years were finished. This is the first resurrection. Blessed and holy is he who has part in the first resurrection. Over such the second death has no power, but they shall be priests of God and of Christ, and shall reign with Him a thousand years.

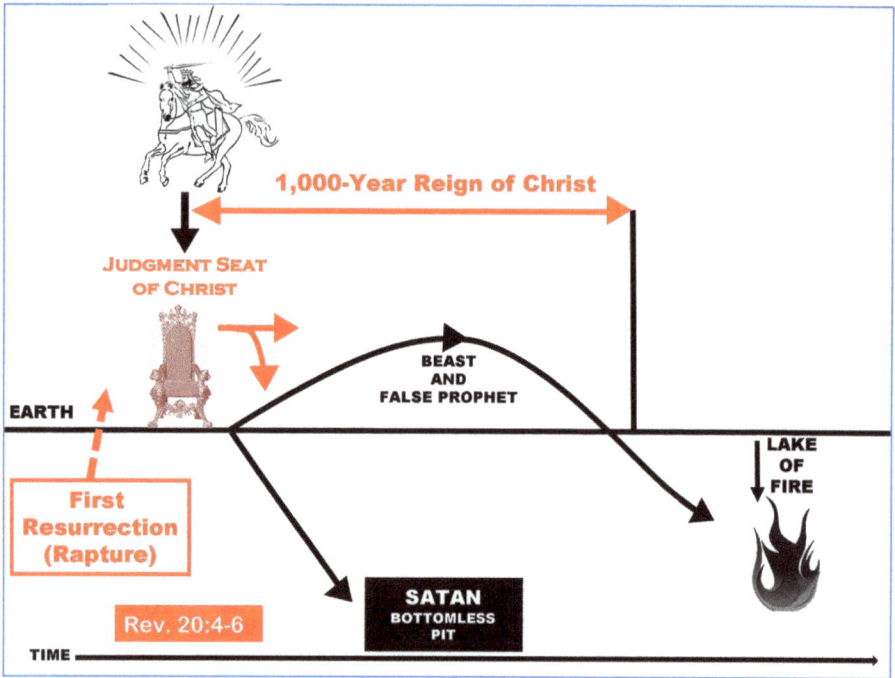

1,000-Year Reign of Christ

JUDGMENT SEAT
OF CHRIST

BEAST
AND
FALSE PROPHET

EARTH

LAKE
OF
FIRE

First
Resurrection
(Rapture)

Rev. 20:4-6

SATAN
BOTTOMLESS
PIT

TIME

There is an amazing amount of information in these passages, so in order not to get bogged down, I'll make a brief overview and come back later to substantiate my assertions. I would suggest that the dotted line represents the First Resurrection, which is the resurrection of the saints. That the "*thrones and judgment was committed to them*" is revealing the Judgment Seat of Christ. Only the saints stand before the Judgment Seat of Christ. We are told: ***"Then I saw the souls of those who had been beheaded for their witness to Jesus and for the word of God, who had not worshiped the beast or his image, and had not received his mark on their foreheads or on their hands. And they lived and reigned with Christ for a thousand years."*** These martyred saints who, by definition, were dead, have arisen in the First Resurrection and are judged worthy to reign with Christ for a thousand years. The implication is that any saints who took the mark would not enter the thousand-year reign of Christ (see Revelation 14:9-12). A judgment is being made as to whether one gets into the thousand-year reign or not. Remember, in Matthew 5 there will be a judgment as to whether a believer goes into Heaven or Hell (Gehenna) based on the condition of one's heart. Some of the resurrected dead enter into the Kingdom, while *"the rest* [or remainder] *of the* [resurrected] *dead did not live again until the thousand years were finished."*

I would suggest that the thousand-year reign is the Kingdom of Heaven, the fullness of Heaven on the earth without evil. Those who are found unworthy to enter into the Kingdom will go to Hell (Gehenna) temporarily, for a thousand years and then resurrect, as we will see further. We will come back and look more deeply into the First Resurrection and the Judgment Seat of Christ after we go through a general overview of the ages.

Right now, let's continue with our timeline:

Revelation 20:7-10

Now when the thousand years have expired, Satan will be released from his prison and will go out to deceive the nations which are in the four corners of the earth, Gog and Magog, to gather them together to battle, whose number is as the sand of the sea. They went up on the breadth of the earth and surrounded the camp of the saints and the beloved city. And fire came down from God out of heaven and devoured them. The devil, who deceived them, was cast into the lake of fire and brimstone where the beast and the false prophet are. And they will be tormented day and night forever and ever.

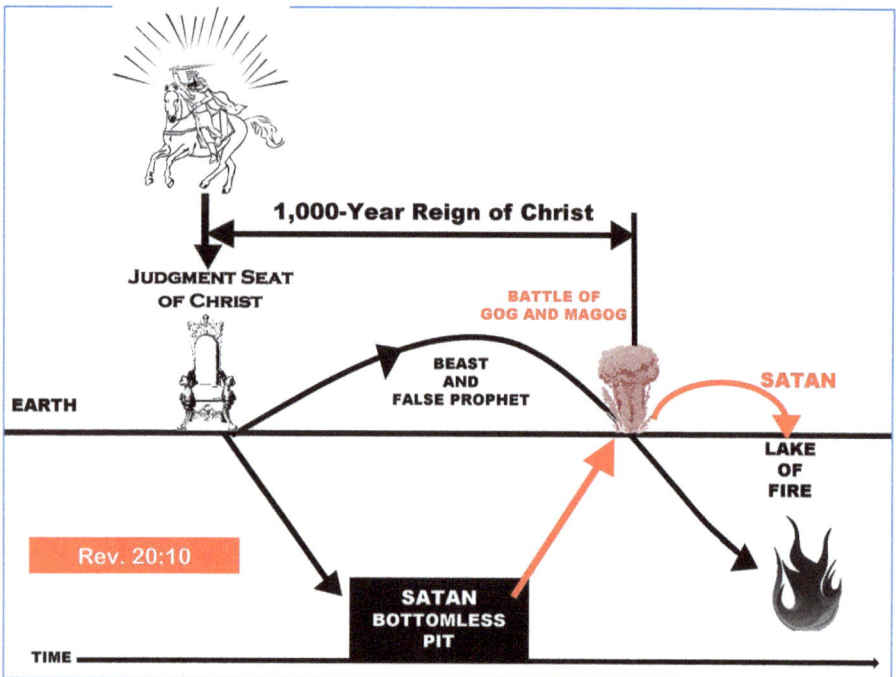

This chart shows the release of Satan from the Bottomless Pit and his arrival on Earth, where he will deceive men and gather an army to fight against the saints and the beloved city. This will be the Battle of Gog and Magog. Fire will be sent down from Heaven by God and will devour the enemy. Satan will then be cast into the Lake of Fire and brimstone, where the Beast and the False Prophets are. They will be tormented day and night forever and ever.

Revelation 20:11-12

Then I saw a great white throne and Him who sat on it, from whose face the earth and the heaven fled away. And there was found no place for them. And I saw the dead, small and great, standing before God, and books were opened. And another book was opened, which is the Book of Life. And the dead were judged according to their works, by the things which were written in the books.

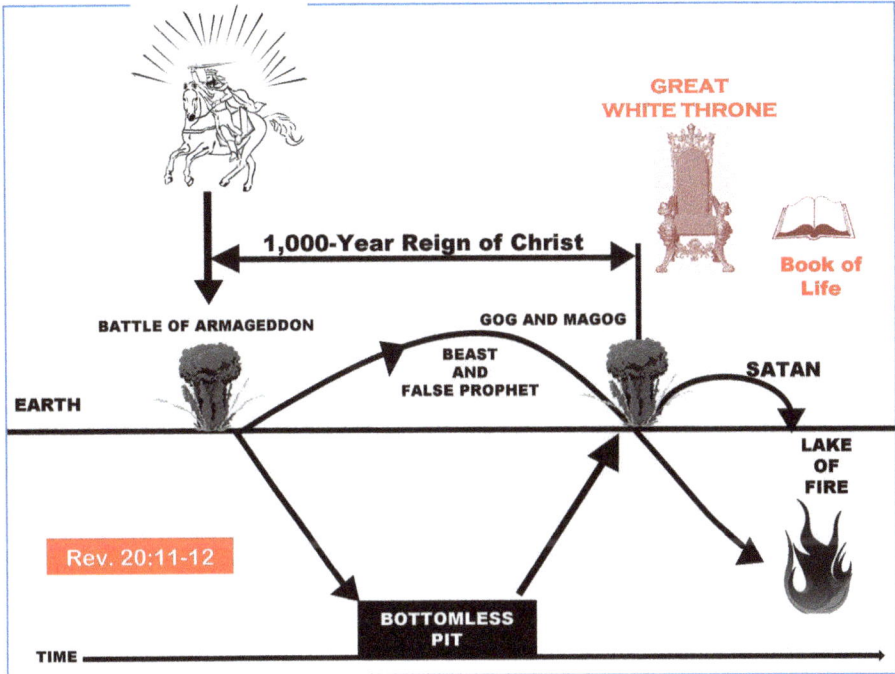

We can see in this chart that what will follow the thousand-year reign of Christ is the Great White Throne Judgment. This will be a display of the awesome power and glory of the Lord, as it is said, *"from whose face the earth and heaven fled away."* This will be like a scene from the Matrix, God on His throne and men and women standing before that throne being judged. Books will be open, and another book, which is the Book of Life.

Revelation 20:13

The sea gave up the dead who were in it, and Death and Hades delivered up the dead who were in them. And they were judged, each one according to his works.

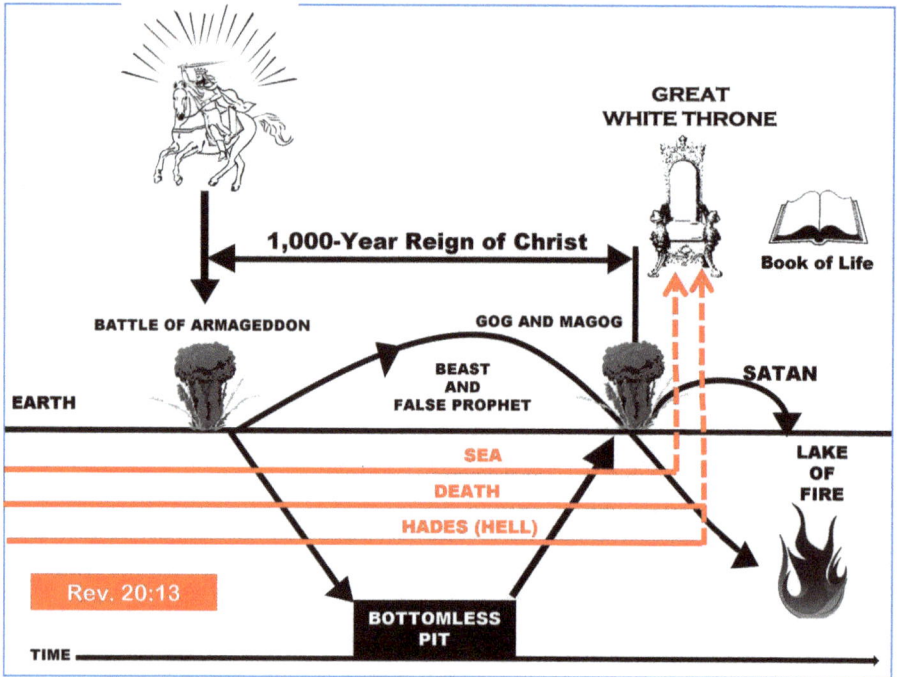

In this chart, we see that the Sea, Death and Hades (Hell) give up their dead to the Great White Throne. The resurrection of the dead is noted by dotted lines and, although it is not specifically stated, this is the second resurrection. The Sea, Death, and Hades represent holding tanks, so to speak for the souls of men and angels that have died and are awaiting final judgment. We will cover these three distinctions further on, but it is important to note that Hades (Hell) is the place where the souls of men are awaiting judgment. The righteous resurrect from Hades (Hell) in the first resurrection, and unbelievers remain in Hades (Hell) until the second resurrection.

Revelation 20:14, KJV

And death and Hell were cast into the lake of fire. This is the second death.

This is an important piece of information. Picture these places, if you will, as giant warehouses containing the souls of the dead, awaiting final judgment. When they are emptied of all the souls in them, these emptied structures are then thrown into the Lake of Fire. It is critical to note that there is a distinction between Hades (Hell) and the Lake of Fire since one is thrown **into** the other. Hades (Hell) will burn forever in the Lake of Fire, but there will be no one in it.

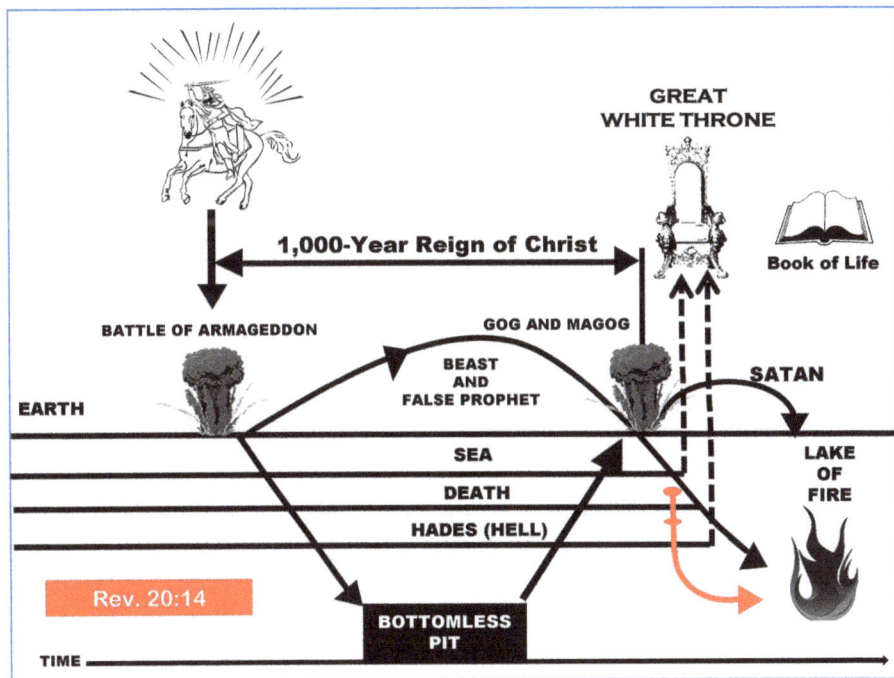

Most of us use *Hell* as a word which communicates eternal wrath, when in fact the Lake of Fire should be used. It is amazing how ingrained this is in our understanding. I still find myself using *Hell* as a description of eternal wrath, even though I've had an understanding to the contrary for years now. You will not understand what Jesus is talking about if you don't SEE this distinction. This is a key to understanding what the Kingdom of Heaven is. Let's continue and focus some more.

Revelation 20:15-21:8

And anyone not found written in the Book of Life was cast into the lake of fire.

Now I saw a new heaven and a new earth, for the first heaven and the first earth had passed away. Also there was no more sea. Then I, John, saw the holy city, New Jerusalem, coming down out of heaven from God, prepared as a bride adorned for her husband. And I heard a loud voice from heaven saying, "Behold, the tabernacle of God is with men, and He will dwell with them, and they shall be His people. God Himself will be with them and be their God. And God will wipe away every tear from their eyes; there shall be no more death, nor sorrow, nor crying. There shall be no more pain, for the former things have passed away." Then He who sat on the throne said, "Behold, I make all things new." And He said to me, "Write, for these words are true and faithful."

And He said to me, "It is done! I am the Alpha and the Omega, the Beginning and the End. I will give of the fountain of the water of life freely to him who thirsts. He who overcomes shall inherit all things, and I will be his God and he shall be My son. But the cowardly, unbelieving, abominable, murderers, sexually immoral, sorcerers, idolaters, and all liars shall have their part in the lake which burns with fire and brimstone, which is the second death."

We see that those who do not have their name in the Book of Life will be cast into the Lake of Fire. Those who have their name in the Book of Life will enter into the next age, which is the New Heaven and New Earth. The New Heaven and New Earth will be eternal, for the scripture states *"there shall be no more death."*

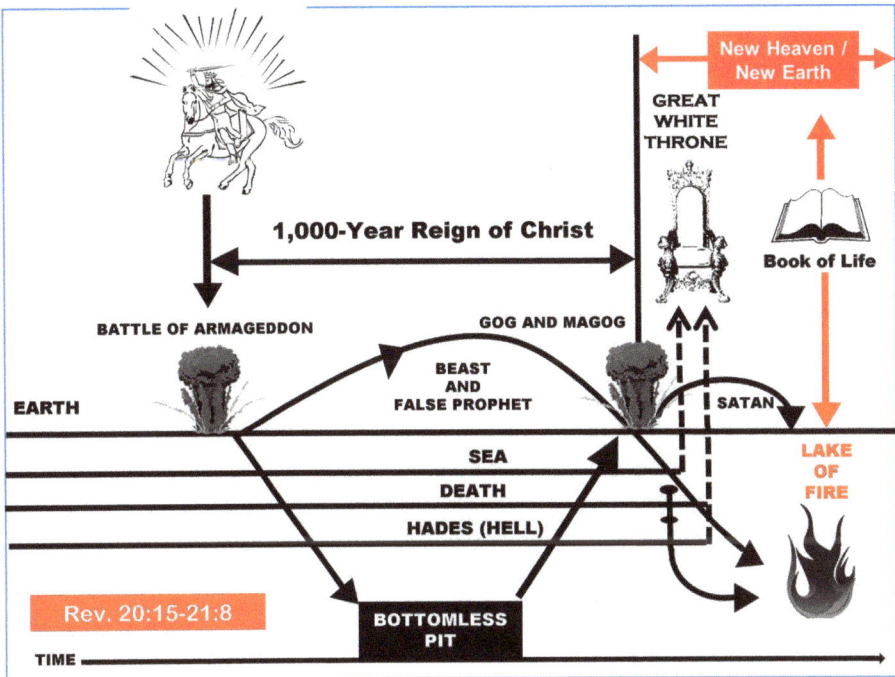

The following chart illustrates the three ages: the present age, the thousand-year reign and the New Heaven and New Earth. We have seen that before each age there is a resurrection of those who are to be judged, to determine whether they will enter into the next age or suffer punishment during that age. The Judgment Seat of Christ will come before the thousand-year reign, and the Great White Throne Judgment will come before the New Heaven and the New Earth.

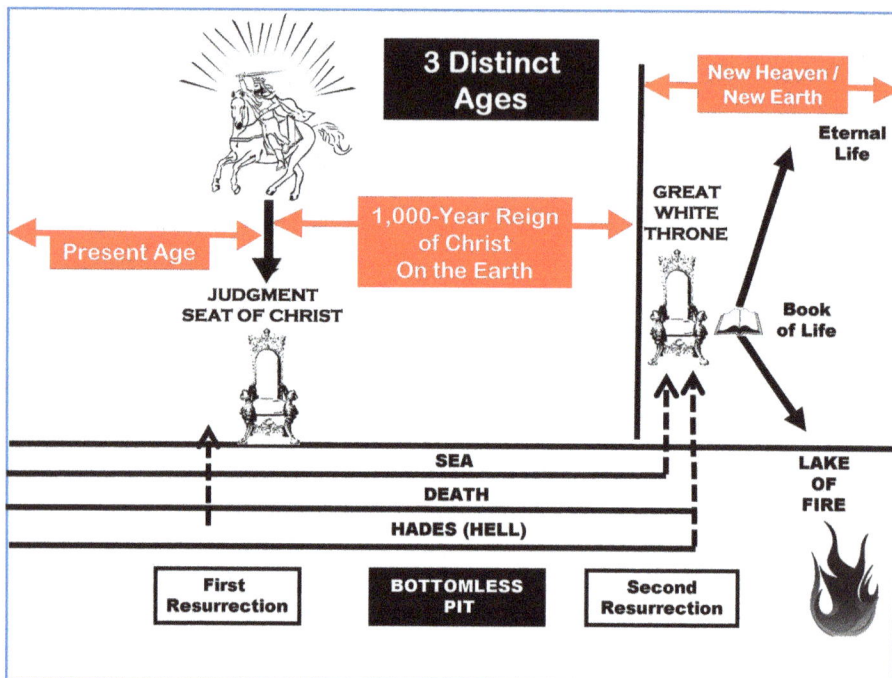

The understanding of these different ages and the distinction of the different judgment seats which precede them may seem insignificant, but they have a profound impact on how people interpret the Scriptures. The vast majority of believers assume that there is just one judgment, so when one dies, they'll either go to Heaven or to the Lake of Fire, and that's it. I would suggest that the understanding of the two judgments and the two coming ages is critical for us to understand how a believer can suffer punishment while also receiving eternal life.

It is when one believes by faith in Christ that our name is written in the Book of Life, and we receive an inheritance of eternal life.

John 3:15

that whoever believes in Him should not perish but have eternal life.

There are two pathways for believers that are determined at the Judgment Seat of Christ (JSOC). Those believers found worthy at the JSOC will enter into the thousand-year reign, after which they will stand before the Great White Throne Judgment (GWTJ) and find their name in the Book of Life, which will allow them to enter the New Heaven and New Earth and receive eternal life. This is designated by the red line.

Those believers found unworthy to enter into the Kingdom of Heaven will suffer in Hell (*Gehenna*) during the thousand years. After that time, those carnal believers will be resurrected before the Great White Throne, during which they will find their names in the Book of Life and receive eternal life in the New Heaven and New Earth. This path is designated by the blue line.

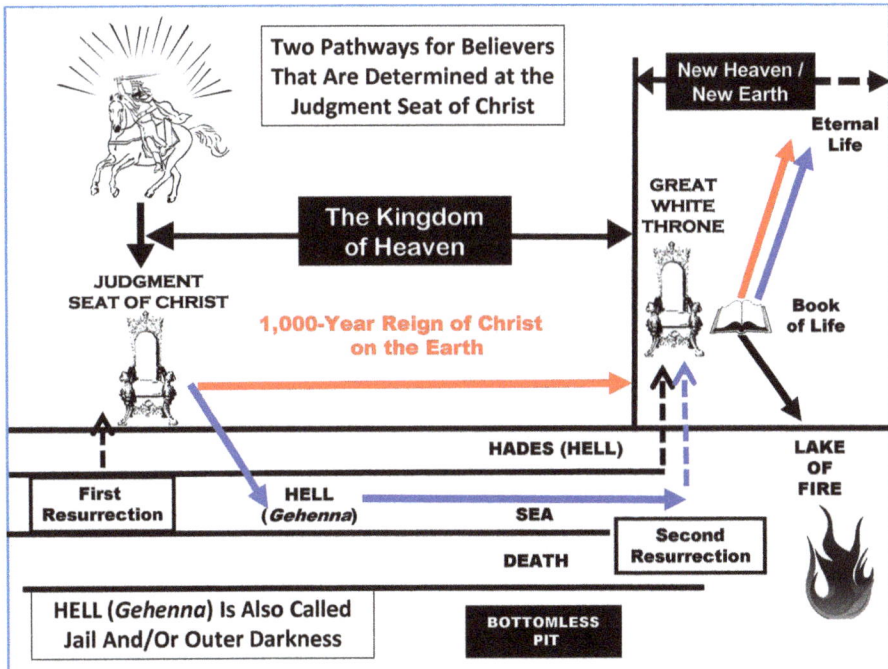

At the end of the thousand-year reign, we see that three places give up their dead:

1.) Hades—also known as Sheol,

2.) Death—also known as Hell (Tartarus), the bottomless pit, and the abyss,

3.) The Sea—also known as Hell (Gehenna), outer darkness, jail.

1.) Hades (Hell) is the place where the souls of men go after they die. This corresponds to Sheol in the Old Testament. Although it may be hard for some to believe, Hades (Hell) is a good place for believers.

We must understand that there are different sections in Hades (Hell). In Luke 16:19-31 Jesus, in telling the Parable of the Rich Man and Lazarus, describes what Hades (Hell) is like. He describes Lazarus as being comforted in Abraham's bosom and the rich man as being in a place of torment from flames. There is a great gulf between these two places, which is impassable. There is much more to say about these passages, but we'll come back to it further on.

Hades (Hell) is the place Jesus descended to and resurrected from. When He told the man beside Him on the cross, *"Today you will be with me in paradise,"* He was talking about Abraham's bosom. Believers will also resurrect from Hades (Hell) at the first resurrection and stand before the JSOC. Unbelievers will resurrect at the second resurrection and stand before the GWTJ.

2.) Death is known as Hell (*Tartarus*), the bottomless pit, and abyss, It is the place where the fallen angels and Satan are held. Hell (*Tartarus*) is used once in the NT in the following scripture:

2 Peter 2:4

For if God did not spare the angels who sinned, but cast them down to hell [tartarus] and delivered them into chains of darkness, to be reserved for judgment ... .

We can see that Hell (*Tartarus*) is a place where the fallen angels are chained awaiting the Final Judgment, which is the Great White Throne

Judgment. They will then be cast into the Lake of Fire, since their names are not in the Book of Life.

Abyssos is translated as "the bottomless pit" or "the abyss" and is used nine times in the NT. Some examples are when Satan is cast into the bottomless pit in Revelation 20:3 and when the demons beg Jesus not to send them to the abyss (see Luke 8:31).

3.) The Sea is also known as Hell (*Gehenna*), outer darkness and jail. Hell (*Gehenna*) is translated nine times as *Hell*, and three times as *Hell fire*. Jesus warned His disciples ten times using Hell (*Gehenna*) as a consequence of living a carnal life. In two cases, Jesus warned the scribes and Pharisees of the consequence of Hell (*Gehenna*) for their hypocritical ways. We should note that the Pharisees had a righteousness that came by faith (Romans 4:3), but in order to enter the Kingdom of Heaven, one's righteousness had to exceed the righteousness that comes from faith (Matthew 5:20), for faith without works is dead (James 2:20).

Jesus never warned unbelievers with Hell (*Gehenna*), only the righteous. Outer darkness is used three times in the NT, and it is a place that believers go after the JSOC. Jail is also used twice in the NT as a place after the judgment of believers. Further study on the "Three 3 Hells" can be found at: www.thekohislike.com.

Hell is a general term that describes any place (good or bad) where souls are awaiting the Final Judgment. The timeline helps us to see that Hell is different from the Lake of Fire.

Throughout the Scriptures, the people of God went astray and committed all manner of wickedness. It was in these times that the prophets were sent forth to warn God's people that, unless they turned and repented there would be all forms of calamity as a consequence of their sins. These consequences have included famine, disease, slaughter in battle, and exile, to name a few. Prophets who declare God's Word to His people have mostly been killed, and so it was with Jesus when He exposed the sins of the scribes and Pharisees.

It has always been the mercy and longsuffering of the Lord to warn us for our own good. The Gospel of the Kingdom is a new covenant, prophetic declaration to the people of God as to how God will judge His people. *"Therefore, repent for the Kingdom of Heaven is at hand"* means that one needs to be ready for the coming of the Lord or else suffer by missing the Kingdom. This is the fear of the Lord.

Make no mistake, justice will be true and exacting, but the great news is that the remedy has been made for everyone who repents. Since the eternal Spirit of God lives in us, the fire of God will only refine us and not destroy us.

Fear the Lord, but don't be afraid. This is not a legalistic, law-driven grind, but a life of knowing the love of God toward us and being transformed into His likeness by the power of the Holy Spirit.

We have covered a lot of ground. I expect you to hold these thoughts loosely and trust that they will be confirmed as we continue our study.

Chapter 4

The Coming Millennial Kingdom

Here is an Old Testament passage which corresponds to the coming of Jesus and the millennial kingdom that we saw in Revelation 19 and 20:

Isaiah 11:1-9

> *There shall come forth a Rod from the stem of Jesse,*
> *And a Branch shall grow out of his roots.*
> *The Spirit of the LORD shall rest upon Him,*
> *The Spirit of wisdom and understanding,*
> *The Spirit of counsel and might,*
> *The Spirit of knowledge and of the fear of the LORD.*
>
> *His delight is in the fear of the LORD,*
> *And He shall not judge by the sight of His eyes,*
> *Nor decide by the hearing of His ears;*
> *But with righteousness He shall judge the poor,*
> *And decide with equity for the meek of the earth;*
> **He shall strike the earth with the rod of His mouth,**
> **And with the breath of His lips He shall slay the wicked.**
> *Righteousness shall be the belt of His loins,*
> *And faithfulness the belt of His waist.*

"The wolf also shall dwell with the lamb,
The leopard shall lie down with the young goat,
The calf and the young lion and the fatling together;
And a little child shall lead them.
The cow and the bear shall graze;
Their young ones shall lie down together;
And the lion shall eat straw like the ox.
The nursing child shall play by the cobra's hole,
And the weaned child shall put his hand in the viper's den.
They shall not hurt nor destroy in all My holy mountain,
For the earth shall be full of the knowledge of the LORD
As the waters cover the sea.*"*

We can see the clear descriptions of Jesus in the first verses, and then, in verse 4, we see that Jesus *"shall strike the earth with the rod of His mouth, and with the breath of His lips He shall slay the wicked."* This will be followed by a time of peace in which the animals live in harmony together, and even a child will not fear a viper. This Kingdom will be on the earth and will cover the earth, as the waters cover the sea.

This next age will be a fulfillment of Old Testament prophecies which foretold that God would reign and dwell with His people Israel on the actual land He gave them. They knew these promises, meditated on them and were anticipating the fulfillment of them.

Ezekiel 37:27-28

My tabernacle also shall be with them; indeed I will be their God, and they shall be My people. The nations also will know that I, the LORD, sanctify Israel, when My sanctuary is in their midst forevermore.

Micah 4:2-4

Many nations shall come and say,
"Come, and let us go up to the mountain of the LORD,

To the house of the God of Jacob;
He will teach us His ways,
And we shall walk in His paths."
For out of Zion the law shall go forth,
And the word of the LORD from Jerusalem.
He shall judge between many peoples,
And rebuke strong nations afar off;
They shall beat their swords into plowshares,
And their spears into pruning hooks;
Nation shall not lift up sword against nation,
Neither shall they learn war anymore.

But everyone shall sit under his vine and under his fig tree,
And no one shall make them afraid;
For the mouth of the LORD of hosts has spoken.

The idea of a coming Kingdom is further seen when Daniel received the interpretation of one of King Nebuchadnezzar's dreams:

Daniel 2:28 and 31-35

But there is a God in heaven who reveals secrets, and He has made known to King Nebuchadnezzar what will be in the latter days. Your dream, and the visions of your head upon your bed, were these:
You, O king, were watching; and behold, a great image! This great image, whose splendor was excellent, stood before you; and its form was awesome. This image's head was of fine gold, its chest and arms of silver, its belly and thighs of bronze, its legs of iron, its feet partly of iron and partly of clay. You watched while a stone was cut out without hands, which struck the image on its feet of iron and clay, and broke them in pieces. Then the iron, the clay, the bronze, the silver, and the gold were crushed together, and became like chaff from the summer

45

threshing floors; the wind carried them away so that no trace of them was found. And the stone that struck the image became a great mountain and filled the whole earth.

The various pieces of this manlike image were representative of the various kingdoms that would be established on the earth over time ... until there would come a Kingdom that would crush the other kingdoms and reign on the earth forever.

Daniel 2:44-45

*And in the days of these kings the God of heaven will set up **a kingdom** which shall never be destroyed; and the **kingdom** shall not be left to other people; it shall break in pieces and consume all these **kingdoms, and it shall stand forever**. Inasmuch as you saw that the stone was cut out of the mountain without hands, and that it broke in pieces the iron, the bronze, the clay, the silver, and the gold — the great God has made known to the king what will come to pass after this. The dream is certain, and its interpretation is sure.*

These are only a small portion of the promises of the coming Kingdom that permeate the Old Testament. Jews yearly celebrate the Feast of Tabernacles, anticipating not only the return of the Messiah, but also that they will tabernacle with Him on the Earth.

This Kingdom is also the inheritance of born-again believers. The promises to Israel are the promises of righteous believers since we have been grafted into the olive tree, which is Israel (see Romans 11:17 and 4:6). We can expect this Kingdom to come, and it is further revealed in the New Testament.

Revelation 20:6

Blessed and holy is he who has part in the first resurrection. Over such the second death has no power, but they shall be priests of God and of Christ, and shall reign with Him a thousand years.

How and when this Kingdom will come has always been a mystery to the people of God, as it is with many today. Even some of Jesus' chosen disciples were confused about why the Son of God would come into the city of Jerusalem on a donkey instead of destroying the Roman Empire with a rod of iron and His breath. When Christ was crucified, did not the disciples begin to question whether or not this was the King of the Kingdom they were expecting?

In many respects modern-day saints have less insight into the coming Kingdom and, thus, are more likely to be caught unaware as to the specific things Jesus said about entering into the Kingdom. Most believers, when asked where we will go after we are resurrected, would say that we go to Heaven. When asked what Heaven will be like, many describe it as an ethereal paradise where saints float through the clouds, play musical instruments and enjoy a tremendous retirement plan. Few would say that, for the first thousand years, we will be ruling and reigning with Jesus on the Earth, yet we'll see that this is exactly what has been prophesied.

CHAPTER 5

WHAT IS THE KINGDOM OF HEAVEN?

Jesus and John the Baptist both exhorted the righteous, *"Repent, for the kingdom of heaven is at hand"* (Matthew 3:1 and 4:17), with clear exhortations to be ready for what was coming next. Jesus was warning that some would not enter the Kingdom of Heaven because of their lawlessness (see Matthew 7:21-23). So what exactly is the Kingdom of Heaven?

Each of the gospels speak of a different characteristic of Jesus. For instance, the book of Matthew speaks of the kingship of Jesus. Interestingly, the *"kingdom of heaven"* is referenced thirty-three times and **only** in the book of Matthew. This book is a valuable resource in describing the coming reign of Christ on the Earth and revealing significant events that will happen as we transition into that age.

The next age will be when Christ rules on the Earth for a thousand years, while Satan is bound in the Abyss. This is when the fullness of the Kingdom of Heaven will be reigning on Earth. It will be on Earth as it is in Heaven at that time.

There is not a direct verse that states that the Kingdom of Heaven is the thousand-year reign, but the following verse can be a piece of the puzzle to affirm that this is indeed the case:

Matthew 5:10

*Blessed are those who are persecuted for righteousness' sake, For theirs is the **kingdom of heaven.***

We saw earlier that the martyrs live and reign with Christ for a thousand years, so we can deduce that the thousand-year reign is the Kingdom of Heaven (if we combine these two scriptures). I know that these scriptures, by themselves, may not be definitive enough for you to believe it, but we will see further verification of this truth as we proceed.

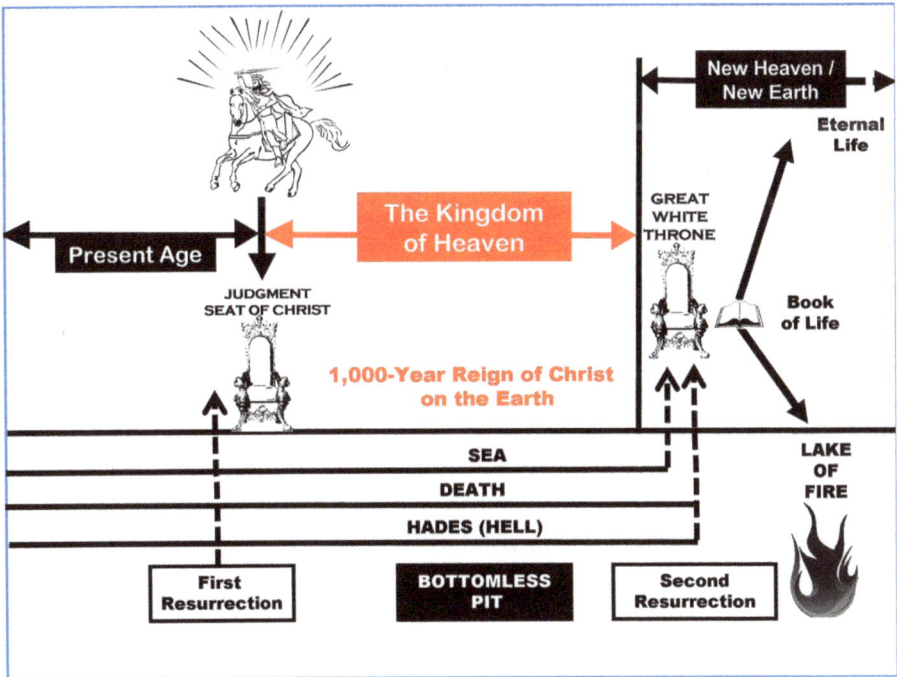

We await and expect the coming Kingdom, but we pray that it would be *"on earth as it is in heaven,"* meaning that we would see the manifestations of Heaven here on Earth as we pray and believe by faith. When Jesus walked on the Earth and signs and wonders were manifest, it was Heaven on Earth. The same is true today when we walk in this Kingdom authority through the Spirit of God. We will look to the parables to give us insight as to when the Kingdom of Heaven actually began.

Matthew 13:31-32

> *Another parable He put forth to them, saying:* ***"The kingdom of heaven is like*** *a mustard seed, which a man took and sowed in his field, which indeed is the least of all the seeds; but when it is grown it is greater than the herbs and becomes a tree, so that the birds of the air come and nest in its branches."*

The *"seed"* of God the Father is Jesus, and the Father sent Jesus to the Earth. Jesus died and was placed into the ground, and from that seed the Kingdom of Heaven came forth.

1 Corinthians 15:36, NLT

> *... When you put a seed into the ground, it doesn't grow into a plant unless it dies first.*

So, the Parable of the Mustard Seed tells us that the Kingdom of Heaven began at the coming of Christ and that it will grow until it surpasses all other trees or kingdoms. This is similar to the interpretation of Daniel's dream that we read earlier. As believers, we expect the coming of the Lord to bring forth the fulness of His reign on the Earth. I have added to our chart a dotted line from the time of Christ on the Earth to the Second Coming of Christ, to illustrate that already-but-not-yet aspect of the Kingdom of Heaven on the Earth.

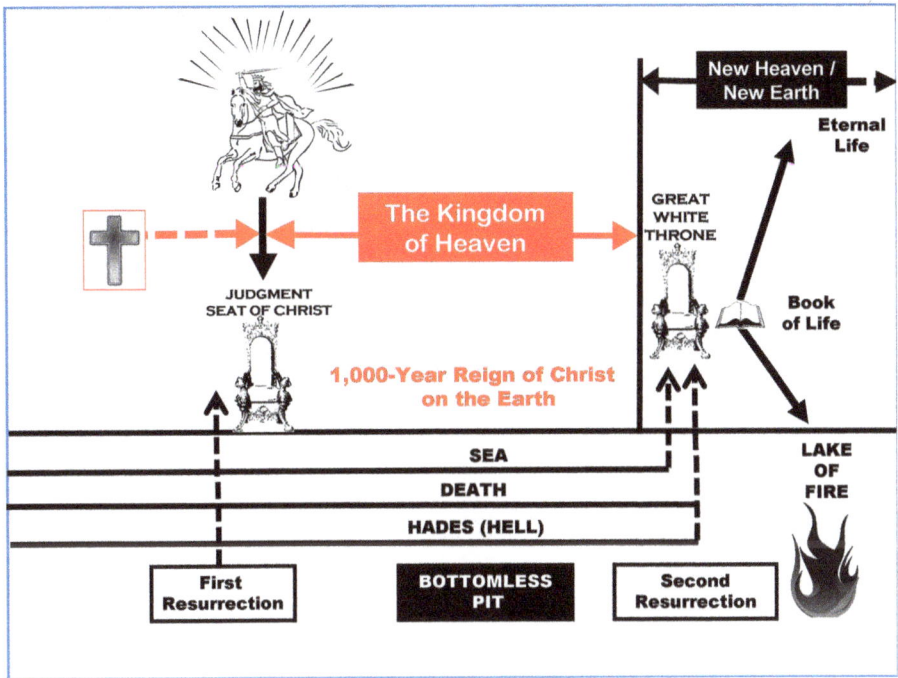

It is important to go over this since we find that the parables are speaking about specific events that will happen as the Kingdom of Heaven approaches. The Parable of the Unforgiving Servant, which begins with, *"the kingdom of heaven is like,"* is showing us the Judgment Seat of Christ, which comes at the start of the Kingdom of Heaven, and there it is determined who will enter into the Kingdom of Heaven.

This may be a good time to show how the Kingdom of Heaven and the Kingdom of God are similar and yet different. Jesus and John the Baptist exhorted the righteous to repent in order to be ready for the coming Kingdom. The book of Matthew states, *"The kingdom of heaven is at hand,"* whiles the other gospels state, *"The kingdom of God is at hand."* Similarly, the parables begin in Matthew with the words, *"The kingdom of heaven is like,"* and the other gospels say, *"The kingdom of God is like."* Why is that?

51

The Kingdom of God includes the beginning and the end (the alpha and the omega) of all time, which means that the arrows move out infinitely in both directions. This includes the present age, the thousand-year reign and the age of the New Heaven and the New Earth. The Kingdom of Heaven in its fullness is **only** the thousand-year reign.

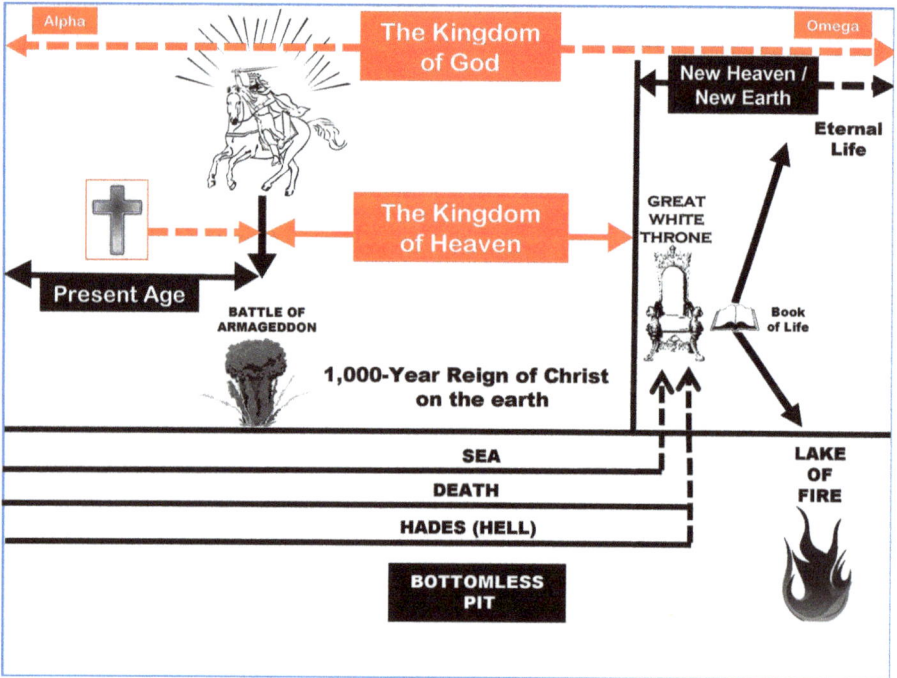

Picture it this way: I could say that something happened in the 1900s, and I could be more specific and say that something happened in the 1930s, and both would be true. This is what is happening here. The Kingdom of God includes all of the Kingdom of Heaven, while the Kingdom of Heaven is only a portion of the Kingdom of God. The parables in the different gospels are the same, which indicates that they are talking about the same time frame. Thus, one could use either the

Kingdom of God or the Kingdom of Heaven, and it would be correct.

This is a key to unlocking the understanding of the Kingdom of Heaven. The parables will illustrate what the resurrection of the saints will be like and what the Judgment Seat of Christ will be like. These events will happen at the end of this age, as the Kingdom of Heaven approaches. Many, when looking at the parables, think that those who are sent to Hell (*Gehenna*) or Outer Darkness are unbelievers, but, in fact, they are believers being judged. Unbelievers will not be judged until the end of the thousand-year reign.

CHAPTER 6

HOW WILL ONE BE JUDGED AT THE JUDGMENT SEAT OF CHRIST?

2 Corinthians 5:9-11a

> *Therefore we make it our aim, whether present or absent, to be well pleasing to Him. For we must all appear before **the judgment seat of Christ**, that each one may receive the things done in the body, according to what he has done, whether good or bad. Knowing, therefore, the terror of the Lord, we persuade men.*

Romans 14:10-12

> *But why do you judge your brother? Or why do you show contempt for your brother? For we shall all stand before the **judgment seat of Christ**. For it is written:*
>
> *"As I live, says the Lord,*
> *Every knee shall bow to Me,*
> *And every tongue shall confess to God."*
>
> *So then each of us shall give account of himself to God.*

1 Peter 1:14-17

*As obedient children, not conforming yourselves to the former lusts, as in your ignorance; but as He who called you is holy, you also be holy in all your conduct, because it is written, "Be holy, for I am holy." And if you call on the Father, who **without partiality judges according to each one's work**, conduct yourselves throughout the time of your stay here in fear.*

Anyone who has stood before a judge can attest to the sober reality of receiving punishment as a consequences of your behavior. This is the fear of the Lord. We will stand before Christ and behold His holiness and purity. His judgments will be true. Nothing will be hidden, for He will be judging the very hearts of men. This is why we need to be ready and understand what will be required of us. All believers will stand before the Judgment Seat of Christ. There will be no unbelievers present.

When we believe in Christ, we become "born again," and the righteousness of Christ is imparted to us.

Philippians 3:9

*And be found in Him, not having my own righteousness, which is from the law, but that which is through faith in Christ, the **righteousness** which is from God by faith.*

Galatians 2:20

I have been crucified with Christ; it is no longer I who live, but Christ lives in me; and the life which I now live in the flesh I live by faith in the Son of God, who loved me and gave Himself for me.

Ephesians 4:24

*And that you put on the new man which was created according to God, in true **righteousness** and holiness.*

2 Corinthians 5:21

*For He made Him who knew no sin to be sin for us, that we might become the **righteousness** of God in Him.*

When we believe by faith, we receive eternal life because the Spirit dwells in us. The Spirit of God is absolutely perfect, holy and eternal. He is the very essence of God. Our spirit man will not be judged, since it is pure and undefiled by definition.

John 3:36

He who believes in the Son has everlasting life; and he who does not believe the Son shall not see life, but the wrath of God abides on him.

1 John 3:9

Whoever has been born of God does not sin, for His seed remains in him; and he cannot sin, because he has been born of God.

This does not mean that when we come to Christ we cannot sin but, rather, that our spirit man cannot sin, for there is no corruption in it.

We are a spirit man, but we also have a soul/body that can sin.

1 John 1:8

If we say that we have no sin, we deceive ourselves, and the truth is not in us.

The following verse was given by Jesus to the disciples after He had told them they would be hated and scorned for His sake.

Matthew 10:28

*And do not fear those who kill the body but cannot kill the soul. But rather fear Him who is able to **destroy both soul and body in hell**.*

Jesus was telling His disciples not to fear man, who could only kill the body, but to fear God, who could destroy both the soul and body in Hell (*Gehenna*). Here we see the separation between the soul/body and the spirit.

The Word of God says *"that each one may receive the things **done** in the body, according to what he has done, whether good or bad"* (2 Corinthians 5:10). Believers will not be seen as perfect. Otherwise there would be no "bad" and no concern about living "unholy" in this life and, most importantly, no reason to repent.

The Lord will be judging our heart/soul/body and will see us the same way He saw the churches in Revelations 2 and 3, with all of their weaknesses and strengths. He called those seven churches to repent eight times and provided a list of consequences they would experience if they failed to obey.

Repentance is certainly part of how we initially became "saved" by faith.

Acts 2:38

Then Peter said to them, "Repent, and let every one of you be baptized in the name of Jesus Christ for the remission of sins; and you shall receive the gift of the Holy Spirit."

Mark 1:15

and saying, "The time is fulfilled, and the kingdom of God is at hand. Repent, and believe in the gospel."

Repentance is also ongoing; it is how we are sanctified. It is the kindness of God that continuously draws us to repentance. Because we have the promise of Christ in us, we are in a dynamic friendship with Him. We are invited to wrestle with the energizing, convicting and very present person of the Holy Spirit, who lives in us. As we turn and return, we are cleansed and restored. As Ed Kurath states, "This is part of the ongoing process of being transformed into the likeness of Jesus."[1]

1 John 1:9

If we confess our sins, He is faithful and just to forgive us our suns and to cleanse us from all unrighteousness.

The opposite is also true. If we don't confess our sins, He won't forgive us our sins, and we won't be cleansed from them. If one has unforgiveness or bitterness in their heart, they have unrighteousness in them and will be judged accordingly. We saw that in the Parable of the Unforgiving Servant. Jesus said that if one has lust in their heart, they will be judged as an adulterer unless they repent.

1 John 2:2, KJV

And he is the propitiation for our sins: and not for ours only, but also for the sins of the whole world.

Jesus has forgiven all the sins of the world—past, present and future—but it is incumbent upon each of us to apply the blood by faith in order for that sacrifice to be effective. The mercies of God are extravagantly given to all who ask without limit. We should never feel condemned with the thought that our sins are too wicked or that we have sinned too much. God will never stop forgiving us! He tells us to forgive our brother seven times seventy in a single day. How much more is His desire to liberally forgive us when we sin! Jesus died so that He could redeem us, restore us and renew us. In fact, it is impossible for us to be good enough without His intervention

1. Edward Kurath, *I Will Give Your Rest* (Post Falls, ID: Divinely Designed, 2003)

When Jesus and John the Baptist exhorted us to *"Repent, for the kingdom of heaven is at hand,"* it was not a burdensome command; it was an invitation to receive the blessings of God. So, although we are righteous by faith, we can do things that are unrighteous that will cause us loss and suffering. This is an exhortation to the righteous.

Romans 6:13

And do not present your members as instruments of unrighteousness to sin, but present yourselves to God as being alive from the dead, and your members as instruments of righteousness to God.

When we stand before the Judgment Seat, we want to be ready by being cleansed from all unrighteousness. Our confidence is that we have a clean heart because we know, by faith, that as we confess our sins, He cleanses us from all iniquity.

Righteous is imputed to those who believe; this includes New Covenant believers and Old Covenant believers alike.

Romans 4:3-5

*For what does the Scripture say? **"Abraham believed God, and it was accounted to him for righteousness."** Now to him who works, the wages are not counted as grace but as debt. But to him who does not work but believes on Him who justifies the ungodly, his faith is accounted for righteousness*

Romans 3:28-30

*Therefore we conclude that a man is justified by faith apart from the deeds of the law. Or is He the God of the Jews only? Is He not also the God of the Gentiles? Yes, of the Gentiles also, since there is one **God who will justify the circumcised by faith and the uncircumcised through faith**.*

59

Romans 4:16

> *Therefore it is of faith that it might be according to grace, so that the promise might be sure to all the seed, not only to those who are of the law, but also to those who are of the faith of Abraham, who is the father of us all.*

Faith was accounted to Abraham as righteousness, and it is through the righteousness of faith that we become the seed of Abraham and inherit the promises made to him.

There is a connection with spiritual Israel (those who believe) that we must embrace, for God sees us all as one.

Romans 11:15-23

> *For if their being cast away is the reconciling of the world, what will their acceptance be but life from the dead? For if the firstfruit is holy, the lump is also holy; and if the root is holy, so are the branches.* **And if some of the branches were broken off, and you, being a wild olive tree, were grafted in among them, and with them became a partaker of the root and fatness of the olive tree, do not boast against the branches. But if you do boast, remember that you do not support the root, but the root supports you.** *You will say then, "Branches were broken off that I might be grafted in." Well said. Because of unbelief they were broken off, and you stand by faith. Do not be haughty, but fear. For if God did not spare the natural branches, He may not spare you either. Therefore consider the goodness and severity of God: on those who fell, severity; but toward you, goodness, if you continue in His goodness. Otherwise you also will be cut off. And they also, if they do not continue in unbelief, will be grafted in,* **for God is able to graft them in again.**

New covenant believers may feel alienated from the saints of old and have a tendency to distance themselves from them, thus disregarding the rich heritage of the root. It is God's desire to make us *"one new man."*

Ephesians 2:12-15

*that at that time you were without Christ, being aliens from the commonwealth of Israel and strangers from the covenants of promise, having no hope and without God in the world. But now in Christ Jesus you who once were far off have been brought near by the blood of Christ. For He Himself is our peace, who has made both one, and has broken down the middle wall of separation, having abolished in His flesh the enmity, that is, the law of commandments contained in ordinances, so as to create in Himself **one new man** from the two, thus making peace.*

I am emphasizing the oneness that we have with Old Covenant believers because that's how God sees us. What has been spoken prophetically to the Jews is instructive to us, since we are connected to them. The promise of the Kingdom of Heaven has been foretold to the Jews, and the Feast of Tabernacles is a dress rehearsal for God's people tabernacling with Him on the earth. These are promises to New Covenant believers as well. There will be a resurrection of the righteous and, I believe, Jew (pre-Jesus) and Gentile will arise together. The righteous will resurrect first and stand before the Judgment Seat of Christ.

Luke 14:14, NIV

*And you will be blessed. Although they cannot repay you, you will be repaid at the **resurrection of the righteous.***

Acts 24:15, NIV

*And I have the same hope in God as these men themselves have, that there will be a **resurrection of both the righteous and the wicked.***

61

There is an inheritance given to believers, which is the thousand-year reign of Christ on the earth. We will see that those believers who are found faithful at the Judgment Seat of Christ will enter into that Kingdom. Those found unworthy will miss it. This is why Jesus exhorted the faithful to be ready by repenting, for the Kingdom of Heaven is at hand.

CHAPTER 7

WHAT WILL HAPPEN TO THOSE WHO MISS THE KINGDOM OF HEAVEN?

Matthew 7:21-23

> *Not everyone who says to Me, "Lord, Lord," shall enter **the kingdom of heaven**, but he who does the will of My Father in heaven. Many will say to Me in that day, "Lord, Lord, have we not prophesied in Your name, cast out demons in Your name, and done many wonders in Your name?" And then I will declare to them, "I never knew you; depart from Me, you who practice lawlessness!"*

"That day" is the Judgment Seat of Christ, which will determine which believers enter into the Kingdom of Heaven. If we let the Scriptures speak for themselves, it is obvious that unbelievers would not be prophesying, casting out demons and doing many wonders **in Christ's name**. Jesus, when accused of casting out demons by the power of Beelzebub, answered this way:

Luke 11:18 and 20

> *If Satan also is divided against himself, how will his kingdom stand? Because you say I cast out demons by Beelzebub.*

But if I cast out demons with the finger of God, surely the kingdom of God has come upon you.

There certainly will be false signs and wonders, but they won't be done by Satan in Jesus' name. Otherwise Satan would be dividing his kingdom. There are some who would say that when Jesus says. *"I never knew you,"* it is an indication that these are not believers. First, Jesus knows everyone. This phrase has to do with intimacy. Most who sin (including believers) stay away from God. Note how Jesus talked to the Laodicean Church that needed to repent.

Revelation 3:19-20

As many as I love, I rebuke and chasten. Therefore be zealous and repent. Behold, I stand at the door and knock. If anyone hears My voice and opens the door, I will come in to him and dine with him, and he with Me.

Jesus was exhorting those in the church to repent, to trust in Him, to open the door to Him and be known by Him. He was saying this because they were separated from Him.

It is hard to reconcile a believer not entering the Kingdom of Heaven ... if we don't understand this to be a distinct age to come that is promised to those believers who are found faithful. The point is that the Lord is not impressed by great displays of the manifestations of the Holy Spirit (miracles, healings and deliverance) if there is lawlessness in that believer's heart. Jesus will be judging the heart and thinks little of the outward appearance.

We saw this in Matthew 5, when Jesus told the one bringing his gift to the altar to set his gift down, be reconciled with his brother, and then bring the gift to the altar.

Matthew 5:20

> *For I say to you, that unless your righteousness exceeds the righteous-ness of the scribes and Pharisees, you will* **by no means enter the kingdom of heaven***.*

I want to challenge you to look at this scripture in a new way. As we saw earlier, there is a righteousness that comes by faith. The Phari-sees were righteous because they believed in God, even though they lived unrighteously. Jesus was saying that your righteousness had to exceed that which comes from just believing. Faith without works is dead. The faith of the Pharisees had become corrupted and, although they looked religious on the outside, God judges the heart. This is a warning to Pharisees in the Church today.

Matthew 23:25 and 27

> *Woe to you, scribes and Pharisees, hypocrites! For you cleanse the outside of the cup and dish, but inside they are full of extortion and self-indulgence.*
> *Woe to you, scribes and Pharisees, hypocrites! For you are like white-washed tombs which indeed appear beautiful outwardly, but inside are full of dead men's bones and all uncleanness.*

If believers who have iniquity in their hearts don't enter the King-dom of Heaven, where do they go?

Matthew 8:8-12

> *The centurion answered and said, "Lord, I am not worthy that You should come under my roof. But only speak a word, and my servant will be healed. For I also am a man under authority, having soldiers under me. And I say to this one, 'Go,' and he goes; and to another, 'Come,' and he comes; and to my servant, 'Do this,' and he does it."*

65

When Jesus heard it, He marveled, and said to those who followed, "Assuredly, I say to you, I have not found such great faith, not even in Israel! And I say to you that many will come from east and west, and sit down with Abraham, Isaac, and Jacob **in the kingdom of heaven. But the sons of the kingdom will be cast out into outer darkness. There will be weeping and gnashing of teeth."**

Here we have Jesus being quite impressed with the faith of a Gentile. This centurion believed that Jesus didn't even have to go to his servant but could just say the words, and the servant would be healed. Jesus stated that He had not seen such great faith in all of Israel. Then Jesus prophesied and said, "*Many will come from the east and the west.*" He was talking about Gentiles coming into the land. They (the Gentiles who have faith) will sit with Abraham, Isaac and Jacob in the Kingdom of Heaven. But the sons of the Kingdom will be cast into Outer Darkness.

The sons of the Kingdom are those who have a right to be there because they have a righteousness that comes by faith. Jesus was confronting the sins of the Pharisees, and they were keenly aware of His accusations.

These verses also show that the Jews and believing Gentiles will share in the inheritance of the Kingdom of Heaven. We see that those who miss the Kingdom of Heaven go into Outer Darkness.

Here is another version from Luke that gives some valuable insights:

Luke 13:24-30

Strive to enter through the narrow gate, for many, I say to you, will seek to enter and will not be able. When once the Master of the house has risen up and shut the door, and you begin to stand outside and knock at the door, saying, "Lord, Lord, open for us," and He will answer and say to you, "I do not know you, where you are from," then you will *begin to say, "We ate and drank in Your presence, and You taught in our streets." But He will say, "I tell you I do not know you, where you are from. **Depart from Me, all you workers of iniquity." There will be weeping and gnashing of teeth**, when you see Abraham and Isaac and Jacob and all the prophets in the kingdom of God, **and yourselves thrust out.** They will come from the east and the west, from the north and the south, and sit down in the kingdom of God. And indeed there are last who will be first, and there are first who will be last.*

We should note that Jesus was talking to the people of God, the righteous. He was not talking to unbelievers. This is a standard prophetic warning that if the workers of iniquity do not repent, they will suffer punishment. This is the Gospel of the Kingdom that is preached to the righteous. Unbelievers don't have the Kingdom to lose since they never had it.

The Master in this story is Jesus, the gate is the way to get into the Kingdom, and that is through the Judgment Seat of Christ. Those who have not repented and, therefore, are workers of iniquity are cast out, and a door is shut on them. It is plain to see from the previous scripture that the place of weeping and gnashing of teeth is the Outer Darkness.

Again we see that those coming from the *"east and the west, from the north and the south, and sit down in the kingdom of God"* is talking about the Gentiles coming into the millennial Kingdom. Now you might guess what this means: *"And indeed there are last who will be first, and there are first who will be last."* The righteous Gentiles who believe in Christ (who are the last to come to faith) may enter into the Kingdom of God before the righteous Jews (who were the first to come to faith).

We see, in Hebrews 3 and 4, that there is a clear warning to New Covenant believers not to follow the ways of those who missed the Promised Land because of their disobedience or unbelief in the wilderness.

Hebrews 3:15-19-4:1

while it is said:

"Today, if you will hear His voice,
Do not harden your hearts as in the rebellion."

For who, having heard, rebelled? Indeed, was it not all who came out
of Egypt, led by Moses? Now with whom was He angry forty years?
Was it not with those who sinned, whose corpses fell in the wilderness?
And to whom did He swear that they would not enter His rest, but to
those who did not obey? So we see that they could not enter in because
of unbelief.
Therefore, since a promise remains of entering His rest, let us fear lest
any of you seem to have come short of it.

This *"rest"* is the inheritance of the thousand-year reign of Christ on the earth for those who are found faithful.

Hebrews 4:11

Let us therefore be diligent to enter that rest, lest anyone fall according
to the same example of disobedience.

Dale Sides shows some interesting parallels in his book, *The 1,000 Year Reign of Jesus Christ on the Earth:*[2]

OLD TESTAMENT	NEW TESTAMENT
Egypt	The world
Pharaoh	Devil
Moses	Jesus Christ
The sea	Water baptism
The cloud	The Holy Spirit

2. http://LMCI.org/The Thousand_Year Reign of Christ

Wilderness	Life
Promised Land	Millennial Kingdom
Crossing the Jordan	Judgment Seat of Christ

Matthew 24:44-51

Therefore you also be ready, for the Son of Man is coming at an hour you do not expect.

Who then is a faithful and wise servant, whom his master made ruler over his household, to give them food in due season? Blessed is that servant whom his master, when he comes, will find so doing. Assuredly, I say to you that he will make him ruler over all his goods. But if that evil servant says in his heart, "My master is delaying his coming," and begins to beat his fellow servants, and to eat and drink with the drunkards, the master of that servant will come on a day when he is not looking for him and at an hour that he is not aware of, and will cut him in two and appoint him his portion with the hypocrites. **There shall be weeping and gnashing of teeth.**

Jesus spoke a very clear exhortation, that His servants must be ready for the coming of the Lord. The Master is the Son of Man, and He will be judging His servants. This is the Judgment Seat of Christ.

We should note that the servant here had an inheritance. He was to rule over all his master's goods. The master was ready to give all of it to the servant ... if he remained faithful and wise. This is the inheritance of ruling and reigning with Christ on the Earth for a thousand years. This servant did evil by beating his fellow servants and eating and drinking with drunkards.

Jesus was poignantly clear that this servant was judged by being cut in two.

Hebrews 4:12

> *For the word of God is living and powerful, and sharper than any*
> *two-edged sword, piercing even to the division of soul and spirit, and*
> *of joints and marrow, and is a discerner of the thoughts and intents*
> *of the heart.*

Who are the hypocrites this evil servant was placed with?

Matthew 23:15 and 33

> *Woe to you, scribes and Pharisees, hypocrites! For you travel land and*
> *sea to win one proselyte, and when he is won, you make him twice as*
> *much a son of **hell** (Gehenna) as yourselves.*
> *Serpents, brood of vipers! How can you escape the condemnation of*
> ***hell** (Gehenna)?*

Matthew 23:13

> *But woe to you, scribes and Pharisees, hypocrites! For you shut up **the***
> ***kingdom of heaven** against men; for you neither go in yourselves, nor*
> *do you allow those who are entering to go in.*

Those who do not enter into the Kingdom go to Hell (*Gehenna*), which is also referred to as Outer Darkness or Jail. This can no longer be confused with the Lake of Fire.

Hebrews 12:14-17

> *Pursue peace with all people, and holiness, without which no one will*
> *see the Lord: looking carefully lest anyone fall short of the grace of*
> *God; lest any root of bitterness springing up cause trouble, and by this*
> *many become defiled; lest there be any fornicator or profane person like*
> ***Esau**, who for one morsel of food sold his birthright. For you know that*

70

afterward, when he wanted to inherit the blessing, he was rejected, for he found no place for repentance, though he sought it diligently with tears.

Esau had a birthright (inheritance) from being the firstborn son, but he sold it to his younger brother Jacob for a bowl of soup. The firstborn was to receive a double portion of the inheritance upon the death of his father. The family name and titles would be passed on through to the firstborn. More significantly, there was a spiritual heritage that would be passed to and through the firstborn, so that the promises of Abraham would continue from generation to generation until this lineage would lead to Christ. Esau was profane in disregarding the precious inheritance he had.

What did it mean for Esau to give up his birthright? He was still a son and would receive the inheritance of a son, but he would no longer receive the double portion that he would normally have received by being the firstborn. He was also disinheriting himself from the spiritual blessings that were his. He was foolish to lose these deep covenant blessings for just a bowl of lentil soup. So let us interpret this scripture with the understanding of the Kingdom of Heaven.

We became children of God when we believed and received an inheritance of a child that cannot be lost (the New Heaven and New Earth). Esau was a son, would always be a son and would, therefore, receive the inheritance of a son. God is faithful to His promises, even when we are unfaithful.

When we believe, we are granted the rights to become the Bride of Christ and enter into the Kingdom of Heaven. This is a birthright that has been given to all who believe. Yet this birthright can be forfeited. Those who love the world can break their bridal vows through their adultery and idolatries and, thus, not enter into the marriage feast. We will see this clearly when we look at the Parable of the Ten Virgins. We saw, in Matthew 7:21-23, that many will not enter the Kingdom of Heaven because

71

of their lawlessness. The riches of this world will fade away like a bowl of lentil soup, and the union with Christ will be lost to those found unprepared at His coming. I can assure you that there will be many saints who will be weeping and gnashing their teeth when they understand the inheritance given to them was lost through their carnality.

For you know that afterward, when he wanted to inherit the blessing, he was rejected, for he found no place for repentance, though he sought it diligently with tears.

The time for repentance will not be at the Day of Judgment; it will be too late then. Repentance must come before we die or before Christ returns. Many will seek repentance diligently with tears, but they will be rejected. This is why there will *"weeping and gnashing of teeth."* It grieves my heart to even say these words, knowing the severity of the Lord and knowing the pure justice that will be executed on the Day of the Lord. This is the fear of the Lord for those who believe. It is this knowledge that compels me to share this message. This is why Jesus said, *"Repent, for the kingdom of heaven is at hand."*

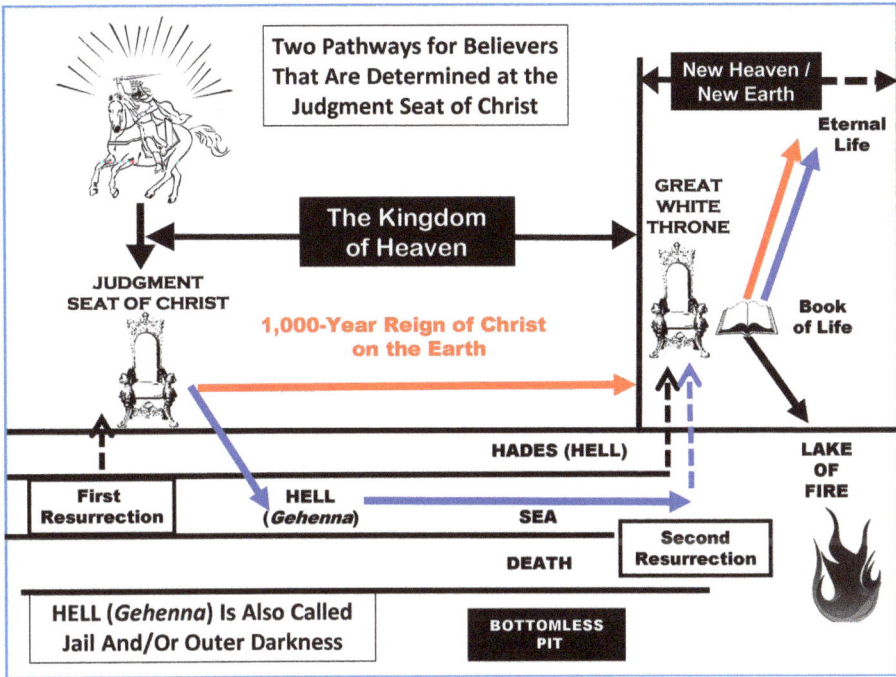

The consequences of not being ready should instill the fear of the Lord into any believer who reads about them, and that was Jesus' intention. A clear warning is a blessing for those who heed it.

Job 28:28

And to man He said,
"Behold, the fear of the LORD, that is wisdom,
And to depart from evil is understanding."

Revelation 21:7

He who overcomes shall inherit all things, and I will be his God and
he shall be My son.

73

1 Corinthians 3:11-15

> *For no other foundation can anyone lay than that which is laid, which is Jesus Christ. Now if anyone builds on this foundation with gold, silver, precious stones, wood, hay, straw, each one's work will become clear; for* **the Day** *will declare it, because it will be revealed by fire; and the fire will test each one's work, of what sort it is. If anyone's work which he has built on it endures, he will receive a reward. If anyone's work is burned, he will suffer loss; but he himself will be saved, yet so as through fire.*

CHAPTER 8

THE TWO INHERITANCES

In the diagram on page 72, there are two inheritances:

1. The Kingdom of Heaven
2. The New Heaven and New Earth.

Let's look at how these two distinguish themselves from each other. **The New Heaven and New Earth** is an inheritance based on faith, and it cannot be lost. It is an inheritance of grace. This is the *"Gospel of grace"*:

Titus 3:4-7

*But when the kindness and the love of God our Savior toward man appeared, **not by works** of righteousness which we have done, but according to His mercy He saved us, through the washing of regeneration and renewing of the Holy Spirit, whom He poured out on us abundantly through Jesus Christ our Savior, that having been justified by His grace we should **become heirs** according to the hope of **eternal life.***

Ephesians 2:8-9

*For by grace you have been saved **through faith**, and that not of yourselves; it is the gift of God, **not of works**, lest anyone should boast.*

John 3:16

> For God so loved the world that He gave His only begotten Son, that whoever **believes** in Him should not perish but have **everlasting life**.

John 3:18 and 36

> He who **believes** in Him is not condemned; but he who does **not believe** is condemned already, because he has **not believed** in the name of the only begotten Son of God.
>
> He who **believes** in the Son has **everlasting life**; and he who does not **believe** the Son shall not see life, but the wrath of God abides on him.

John 6:40 and 47

> And this is the will of Him who sent Me, that everyone who sees the Son and **believes** in Him may have **everlasting life**; and I will raise him up at the last day.
>
> Most assuredly, I say to you, he who **believes** in Me has **everlasting life**.

John 11:25

> Jesus said to her, "I am the resurrection and the life. He who **believes** in Me, though he may die, **he shall live**."

Romans 10:10

> For with the heart one **believes** unto righteousness, and with the mouth confession is made unto salvation.

Romans 4:5-6

> But to him who does not work but **believes** on Him who justifies the ungodly, his faith is accounted for righteousness, just as David also describes the blessedness of the man to whom God imputes righteousness apart from works.

The Kingdom of Heaven is an inheritance that is based on repentance and obedience to the Word of God. This is the Gospel of the Kingdom:

1 Thessalonians 5:23

Now may the God of peace Himself sanctify you completely; and may your whole spirit, soul, and body be preserved blameless at the coming of our Lord Jesus Christ.

Revelation 22:12

And behold, I am coming quickly, and My reward is with Me, to give to every one according to his work.

Hebrews 10:37-39, NLT

"For in just a little while,
* the Coming One will come and not delay.*
And my righteous ones will live by faith.
* But I will take no pleasure in anyone who turns away."*

But we are not like those who turn away from God to their own destruction. We are the faithful ones, whose souls will be saved.

2 Peter 1:10-11

Therefore, brethren, be even more diligent to make your call and election sure, for if you do these things you will never stumble; for so an entrance will be supplied to you abundantly into the everlasting kingdom of our Lord and Savior Jesus Christ.

2 John 1:8

Look to yourselves, that we do not lose those things we worked for, but that we may receive a full reward.

Matthew 10:28

And do not fear those who kill the body but cannot kill the soul. But
rather fear Him who is able to destroy both soul and body in hell.

Believers will stand before the Judgment Seat of Christ and be evaluated as to the life they have lived. Those found faithful will enter the Kingdom of Heaven and not suffer punishment.

Now, let's look at a chart that was put together by **Dale Sides.**[3] It illustrates the differences between these two inheritances:

---

3. http://LMCI.org/The Thousand_Year Reign of Christ

Inheritances of the Kingdoms

Inheritance of the New Heavens and Earth	Inheritance of the Millennial Kingdom
Salvation of the spirit	Salvation of the soul
Kingdom of the Father (Matthew 13:43)	Kingdom of the Son (Colossians 1:13)
Inheritance of a child (Romans 8:17)	Inheritance of a son (Romans 8:17)
By grace (Titus 3:7; Ephesians 2:8)	By obedience to the Word of God (James 1:21)
Accomplished reality for a Christian	Presently being accomplished by a Christian
Achieved by believing (John 3:16)	Achieved by repenting (Matthew 3:2, 4:17)
Cannot be lost (1 Peter 1:4)	Can be lost (Proverbs 14:14; 2 John 8)
Specific to the gospel of John	Specific to the gospel of Matthew
Milk of the Word of God (Hebrews 5:13)	Meat of the Word of God (Hebrews 5:14)

Let's see these two inheritances together in the same verse:

Romans 8:16-17

*The Spirit Himself bears witness with our spirit that we are children of God, and if children, then heirs—**heirs of God and joint heirs with***

79

Christ, if indeed we suffer with Him, that we may also be glorified together.

When we believe by faith, we become a child of God the Father and become His heir. This inheritance is eternal life and the New Heaven and New Earth.

We become joint heirs with Christ **if** we indeed suffer with Him. This inheritance is conditional upon whether or not we suffer with Him, whether we overcome the pain of suffering that comes from being rejected and that we humble ourselves and love our enemies, etc. Suffering is not required of children; it is an attribute of a disciple growing in maturity.

Discipline requires suffering (foregoing pleasure), to be trained to a particular end. This is not something children can do until they have grown and matured. The benefit of suffering with Christ is to be glorified with Him in the Kingdom of Heaven. The opposite will be true for those who don't suffer; they will not be glorified with Christ and will suffer the loss of an inheritance that could have been theirs.

As we have seen, we become born again, or righteous, when we believe, and yet there is a righteousness that we receive when we obey and do God's will.

1 John 3:7

Little children, let no one deceive you. He who practices righteousness is righteous, just as He is righteous.

Revelation 19:8

And to her it was granted to be arrayed in fine linen, clean and bright, for the fine linen is the righteous acts of the saints.

James 2:21-22

Was not Abraham our father justified by works when he offered Isaac his son on the altar? Do you see that faith was working together with his works, and by works faith was made perfect?

I want to share here another excerpt from Ed Kurath's book entitled *I Will Grant You Rest*:[4]

A subtle but profound misunderstanding of what we are like inside has made it difficult for many Christians to see how there can be sin inside us. There is a prevalent view that implies that inside we are like a jar, a container with a single compartment. Therefore, when we give our life to Jesus, He forgives our sins and the jar is now clean. Now that we are pure on the inside, we should be able to act pure on the outside.

The reason this view is erroneous is that, unfortunately, this is *never* the way it works. I know of no one, including myself, for whom life has been this way. And it was not that way for Paul when he wrote the book of Romans (specifically chapter 7:15-17) for us.

The truth is that inside we are more like a honeycomb than a honey jar. We have many compartments, not just one. Some of the compartments contain Jesus, and those are like the "good roots" referred to in Scripture; good roots produce good fruit.

Galatians 5:22-23

But the fruit of the Spirit is love, joy, peace, longsuffering, kindness, goodness, faithfulness, gentleness, self-control. Against such there is no law.

---

4. Edward Kurath, *I Will Give You Rest* (Post Falls, ID: Divinely Designed,2003)

Matthew 7:17-18 and 20

Even so, every good tree bears good fruit, but a bad tree bears bad fruit. A good tree cannot bear bad fruit, nor can a bad tree bear good fruit. Therefore by their fruits you will know them.

However, some of the compartments still contain bad roots. These bad roots produce bad fruit, and they are still present and continue to produce bad fruit even after we become a Christian. Picture these dark spots as areas we need to bring Jesus into. This transformation is a process, not a one-time event.

This is the sanctification process which is addressed in so many places in the Bible. Bringing Jesus into each compartment is the process of being changed into His image.

Once Jesus has taken up residence in that particular place in our "honeycomb," He produces the good fruit automatically, because Jesus can do nothing but produce good fruit.

What Ed has presented here is an excellent way to picture how sanctification happens in us. I might add that his book goes into greater detail in identifying those "bad roots" and the transformation process that brings healing to the inner man. This can all happen without the aid of sackcloth and ashes.

When we humble ourselves and confess our sins before the Lord, we experience the supernatural work of the Spirit, which removes guilt and shame, cleanses us from all iniquity and transforms our stony hearts into hearts of flesh. We experience the transforming presence of God so that we are confident in His love for us. Repentance is a good thing.

CHAPTER 9

THE FIRST RESURRECTION

Now, let's revisit the First Resurrection, which will take place before the Judgment Seat of Christ.

1 Thessalonians 4:16-17

For the Lord Himself will descend from heaven with a shout, with the voice of an archangel, and with the trumpet of God. And the dead in Christ will rise first. Then we which are alive and remain shall be caught up together with them in the clouds, to meet the Lord in the air: and so shall we ever be with the Lord.

The dead in Christ will rise first, followed by those in Christ who are alive on the Earth and will meet Christ in the air. Some would understand this as the Rapture of the saints, but to be consistent with biblical terminology, we will use the term Resurrection, specifically the First Resurrection.

Matthew 24:29-31

Immediately after the tribulation of those days the sun will be darkened, and the moon will not give its light; the stars will fall from heaven, and the powers of the heavens will be shaken. Then the sign of the Son of Man will appear in heaven, and then all the tribes of the earth will mourn, and they will see the Son of Man coming on the clouds of heaven with power and great glory. And He will send His angels with a great sound of a trumpet, and they will gather together His elect from the four winds, from one end of heaven to the other.

We should note here that this is the first appearing of the Son of Man since His resurrection, and He will come with His angels and a great sound of the trumpet. The elect will be gathered by the angels (which is important to note as we interpret the parables). The saints will meet Jesus in the sky at the Resurrection. This is different from when Jesus descends to the Earth at the Battle of Armageddon. This comes later, as we can see in the following diagram.

Where will we land when we resurrect?

Ezekiel 37:11-12

Then He said to me, "Son of man, these bones are the whole house of Israel. They indeed say, 'Our bones are dry, our hope is lost, and we ourselves are cut off!' "Therefore prophesy and say to them, 'Thus says the Lord GOD: "Behold, O My people, I will open your graves and cause you to come up from your graves, and bring you into the land of Israel."'"

We see that Israel will be resurrected onto the **"land of Israel,"** the actual *terra fima*. This is a critical point which is lost by many. Israel (which we have been grafted into) will be resurrected onto the land given to us by God. This makes sense since the Kingdom of Heaven will be on the earth, and the throne on God will be established in Jerusalem (see Jeremiah 3:17). We will be following the pattern that has been established by Jesus. Jesus died, He went to Hades (Paradise) and then resurrected from the dead. And where did He land? Jerusalem. I trust we will follow this same pattern. In upcoming chapters we will see what happens after we land.

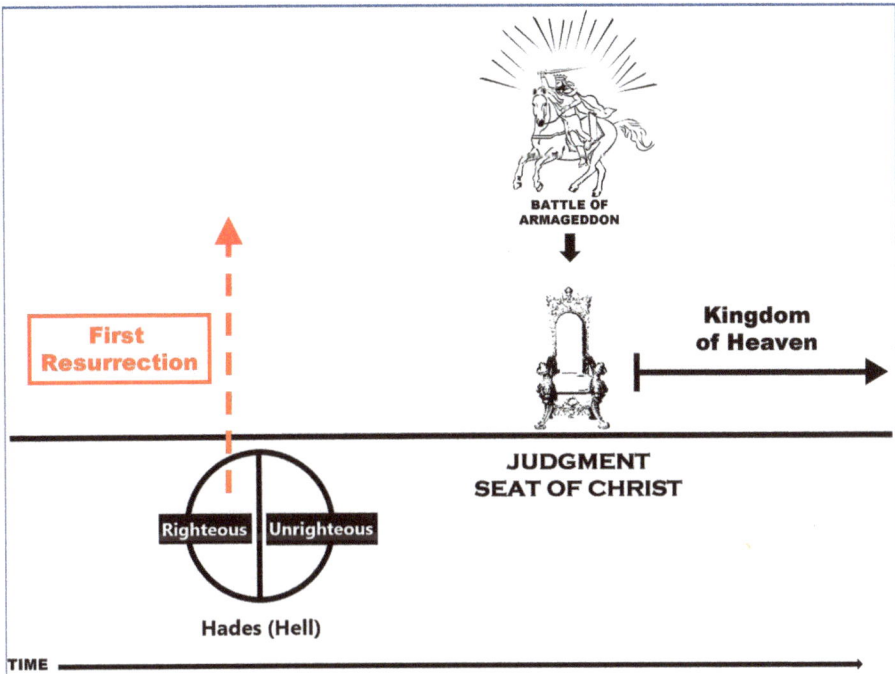

We will look at the parables which reveal how the Kingdom will unfold, starting at the Resurrection, the Wedding, the Judgment Seat of Christ and more. Some of the parables will be describing the same event but will use different imagery. Remember, we are trying to solve a mystery!

CHAPTER 10

THE PARABLE OF THE TEN VIRGINS

The Parable of the Ten Virgins speaks of what will transpire at the Resurrection:

Matthew 25:1-13

Then the **kingdom of heaven** *shall be likened to ten virgins who took their lamps and went out to meet the bridegroom. Now five of them were wise, and five were foolish. Those who were foolish took their lamps and took no oil with them, but the wise took oil in their vessels with their lamps. But while the bridegroom was delayed, they all slumbered and slept.*

And at midnight a cry was heard: "Behold, the bridegroom is coming; go out to meet him!" Then all those virgins arose and trimmed their lamps. And the foolish said to the wise, "Give us some of your oil, for our lamps are going out." But the wise answered, saying, "No, lest there should not be enough for us and you; but go rather to those who sell, and buy for yourselves." And while they went to buy, the bridegroom came, and those who were ready went in with him to the wedding; and the door was shut.

Afterward, the other virgins came also, saying, "Lord, Lord, open to us!" But he answered and said, "Assuredly, I say to you, I do not know you."

Watch therefore, for you know neither the day nor the hour in which the Son of Man is coming.

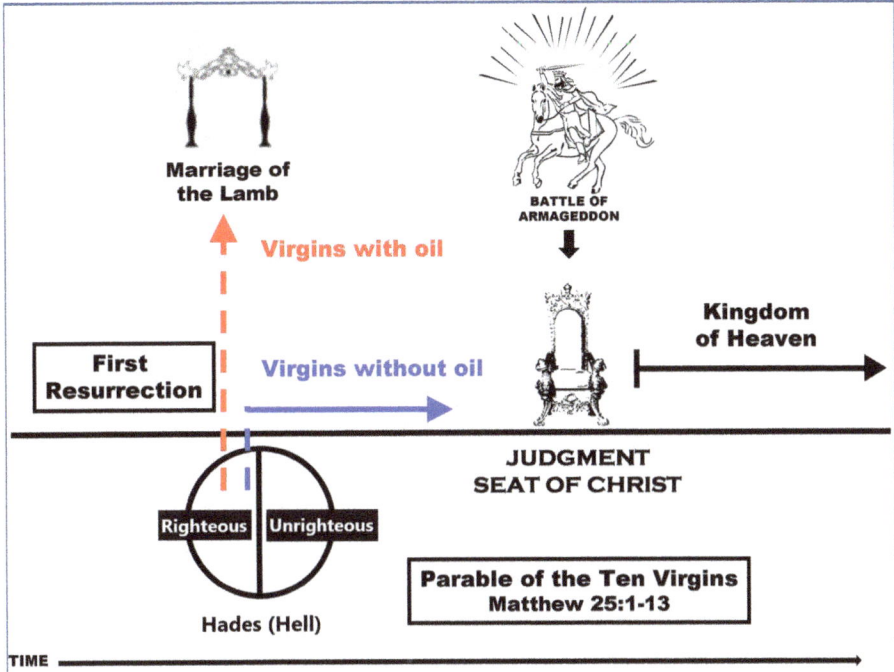

The virgins represent purity; you cannot be a 90% virgin because then you would not be a virgin at all. Righteousness is the same; anything less than righteous is unrighteous. Born-again believers are filled with the Spirit of God, the righteousness of God.

The ten virgins are symbolic of believers, who, like these virgins, have a purity about them (righteousness) yet can make bad choices that have consequences. Five of them were ready to meet the Bridegroom (Jesus), but five were not. Those who were ready had their lamps filled with extra oil and entered into the wedding feast. The ones who were not ready were left outside the shut door shouting, *"Lord, Lord, open to us!"* Does this sound like a cry from unbelievers? Would unbelievers be going out to meet the Bridegroom?

An important point to note here is that the virgins fell asleep and then *"arose"* at the coming of the Bridegroom. In other scriptures, falling asleep is used as a way to communicate someone dying. The virgins arising represents the Resurrection from the dead. Traditionally, when the bridegroom approached the bride, a member of his party would blow the shofar. This is analogous to Christ coming with the blowing of the trumpet and meeting His Bride in the air.

In the previous diagram, I have shown the wedding canopy (*chuppah* or *huppah*), which is where a Jewish wedding ceremony is performed.

Where does the Bride go?

Revelation 14:1-5

Then I looked, and behold, **a Lamb standing on Mount Zion, and with Him one hundred [and] forty-four thousand,** *having His Father's name written on their foreheads. And I heard a voice from heaven, like the voice of many waters, and like the voice of loud thunder. And I heard the sound of harpists playing their harps. They sang as it were a new song before the throne, before the four living creatures, and the elders; and no one could learn that song except the hundred [and] forty-four thousand who were redeemed from the earth. These are the ones who were not defiled with women, for* **they are virgins.** *These are the ones who follow the Lamb wherever He goes.* **These were redeemed from [among] men, [being] firstfruits to God and to the Lamb.** *And in their mouth was found no deceit, for they are without fault before the throne of God.*

This seems to be picture of the Bride. It is unclear whether there will be exactly 144,000, or if this number represents completion by the correlation of 12,000 from each of the twelve tribes. We might note that Psalm 45:14 states that royal Bride will be *followed by her virgin brides-maids,"* thus the virgins could be referencing the Bride and/or bridal party. Be that as it may, we see that these pure virgins will be standing on Mount Zion with Jesus at the end of the age.

Here is the description of the wedding:

Revelation 19:6-9

And I heard, as it were, the voice of a great multitude, as the sound of many waters and as the sound of mighty thunderings, saying, "Alleluia! For the Lord God Omnipotent reigns! "Let us be glad and rejoice and give Him glory, for the marriage of the Lamb has come, and His wife has made herself ready." **And to her it was granted to be arrayed in fine linen, clean and bright, for the fine linen is the righteous acts of the saints.** *Then he said to me, "Write: 'Blessed [are] those who are called to the marriage supper of the Lamb!'" And he said to me, "These are the true sayings of God."*

Here is a description of Jesus descending from the heights to the earth to do battle:

Revelation 19:11-1

Now I saw heaven opened, and behold, a white horse. And He who sat on him [was] called Faithful and True, and in righteousness He judges and makes war. His eyes [were] like a flame of fire, and on His head [were] many crowns. He had a name written that no one knew except Himself. He [was] clothed with a robe dipped in blood, and His name is called The Word of God. **And the armies in heaven, clothed in fine linen, white and clean, followed Him on white horses.** *Now out of His mouth goes a sharp sword, that with it He should strike the nations. And He Himself will rule them with a rod* *of iron. He Himself treads the winepress of the fierceness and wrath of Almighty God.*

Note that the Bride/Bridesmaids are dressed in *"fine linen, white and clean"* and those who descend with Christ are dressed in *"fine linen, white and clean."* I would suggest that the Bride/Bridesmaids follow Jesus into the Battle of Armageddon. This battle is followed by the Judgment Seat of Christ. This is the transition from this age into the Kingdom of Heaven.

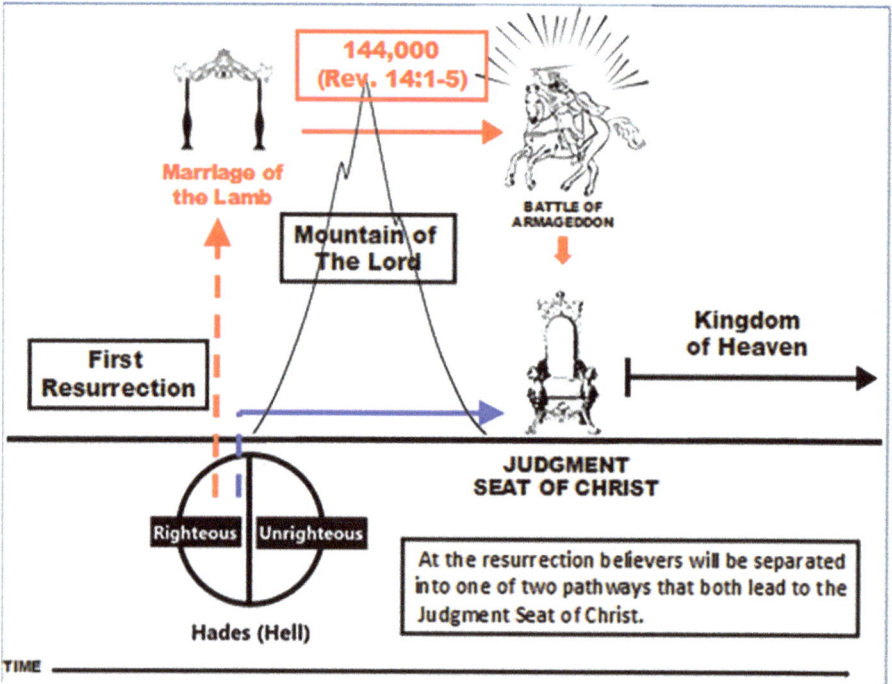

Although there is a separation of the righteous at the Resurrection, this is not the Judgment Seat of Christ. The virgins with the oil take the red route, and the virgins without oil take the blue route. We will talk about this time between the Resurrection and the Judgment Seat in greater detail further on. Now we will look at two more parables which illustrate the separation that happens at the Resurrection.

CHAPTER 11

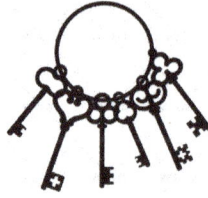

THE PARABLE OF THE DRAGNET

Matthew 13:47-50

*Again, the **kingdom of heaven is like** a dragnet that was cast into the sea and gathered some of every kind, which, when it was full, they drew to shore; and they sat down and gathered the good into vessels, but threw the bad away. So it will be at the end of the age. The angels will come forth, separate the wicked from among the just, and cast them into the furnace of fire. There will be wailing and gnashing of teeth.*

In the following diagram, we see that the dragnet was cast into the sea and then pulled back to shore when it was full. This pulling up of the net speaks of the Resurrection. The net being full speaks of the *"fullness of the gentiles"* and the appointed time set for harvest. The angels will then separate the good from the bad and place each in their appropriate places. The good will be placed into vessels, and the bad into the *"furnace of fire."* Note the similarities in what the angels do from a previous scripture we looked at.

Matthew 24:31

*And He will send **His angels** with a great sound of a trumpet, and **they will gather together His elect** from the four winds, from one end of heaven to the other.*

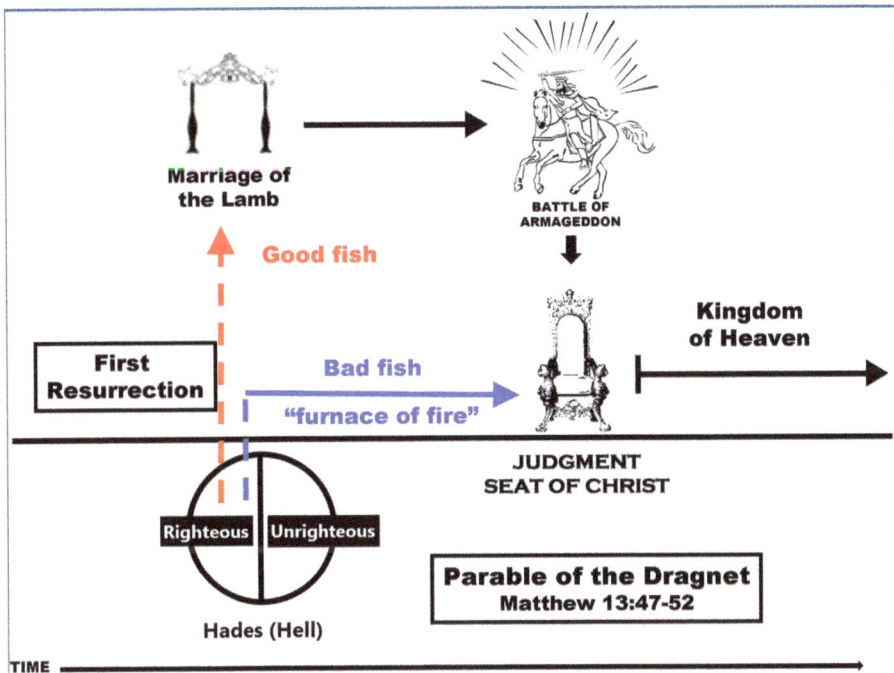

Now let's look further into Matthew 13:49:

Matthew 13:49

So it will be at the end of the age. The angels will come forth, separate the wicked from among the just.

This is talking about the Resurrection at the end of this age, the Resurrection of the righteous. It is not talking about the Second Resurrection since that comes in the next age. This is crucial. The wicked are separated *"from among the just,"* again revealing that this is the First Resurrection. This parallels the separation that will happen between the virgins that have oil and those who do not.

John 5:26-29, NASB

> *For just as the Father has life in Himself, even so He gave to the Son also to have life in Himself; and He gave Him authority to execute judgment, because He is the Son of Man. Do not marvel at this; for an hour is coming, in which all who are in the tombs will hear His voice, and will come forth; those who did the good deeds to a resurrection of life, those who committed the evil deeds to a resurrection of judgment.*

Now, let's move on to the next parable that also speaks of the Resurrection.

CHAPTER 12

THE PARABLE OF THE WHEAT AND TARES

Matthew 13:24-30 and 36-43

Another parable He put forth to them, saying: **"The kingdom of heaven is like** *a man who sowed good seed in his field; but while men slept, his enemy came and sowed tares among the wheat and went his way. But when the grain had sprouted and produced a crop, then the tares also appeared. So the servants of the owner came and said to him, 'Sir, did you not sow good seed in your field? How then does it have tares?' He said to them, 'An enemy has done this.' The servants said to him, 'Do you want us then to go and gather them up?' But he said, 'No, lest while you gather up the tares you also uproot the wheat with them. Let both grow together* **until the harvest, and at the time of harvest** *I will say to the reapers, "First gather together the tares and bind them in bundles to burn them, but gather the wheat into my barn."'"*

Then Jesus sent the multitude away and went into the house. And His disciples came to Him, saying, "Explain to us the parable of the tares of the field." He answered and said to them: "He who sows the good seed is the Son of Man. The field is the world, the good seeds are the sons of the kingdom, but the tares are the sons of the wicked one. The enemy who sowed them is the devil, **the harvest is the end of the age, and the reapers are the angels.** *Therefore as the tares are gathered and* *burned in the fire, so it will be at the end of this age. **The Son of Man will send out His angels,** and they **will gather out of His kingdom all things that offend, and those who practice lawlessness,** and **will cast them into the furnace of fire.** There will be wailing and gnashing of teeth. Then the righteous will shine forth as the sun in the kingdom of their Father. He who has ears to hear, let him hear!"*

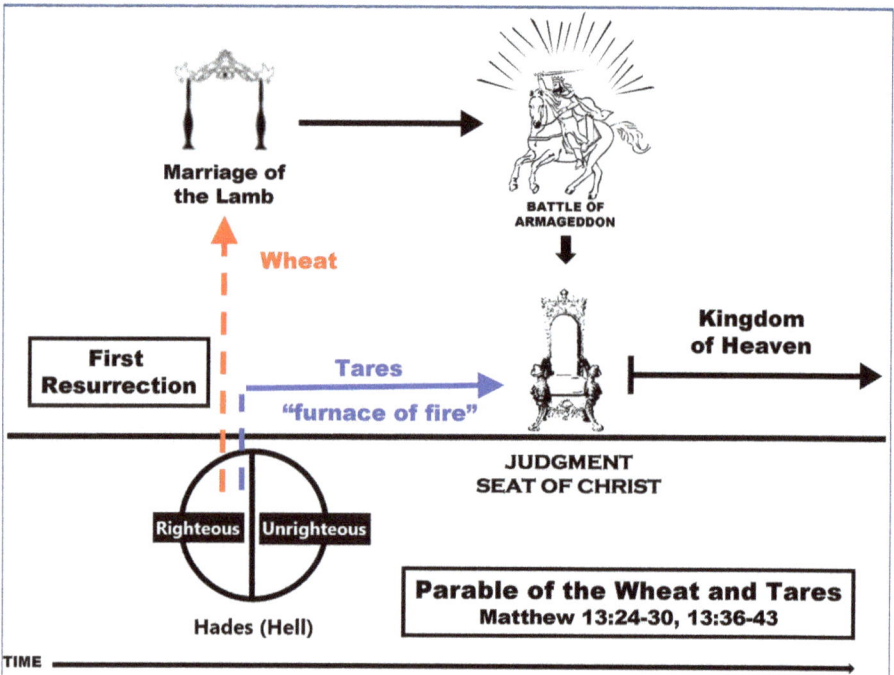

Marriage of the Lamb

BATTLE OF ARMAGEDDON

Wheat

First Resurrection

Tares

"furnace of fire"

Kingdom of Heaven

JUDGMENT SEAT OF CHRIST

Righteous | Unrighteous

Hades (Hell)

Parable of the Wheat and Tares
Matthew 13:24-30, 13:36-43

TIME

Again, we can see that the angels are the reapers, and the harvest is at the end of the age. We see that the angels will "*gather **out of His kingdom** all things that offend, and those who practice lawlessness.*" It may seem that the tares are unbelievers, because it says, "*the tares are the sons of the wicked one.*" Satan does not create; he can only corrupt that which God has already created. The seeds that he sows are temptations, and those seeds can bear the fruit of corruption.

2 Timothy 2:26

And that they may come to their senses and escape the snare of the devil, having been taken captive by him to do his will.

John 8:44

You are of your father the devil, and the desires of your father you want to do. He was a murderer from the beginning, and does not stand in the truth, because there is no truth in him. When he speaks a lie, he speaks from his own resources, for he is a liar and the father of it..

In the Church (*ecclesia*) today, there are those who are scribes and Pharisees (tares), and they will suffer for it. There are also those who are living unto God (wheat), and they will receive a great reward. The tares will be cast into the *"furnace of fire,"* and this is considered by some to be an indication that they are unbelievers. But this is not the case; this fire is different from the Lake of Fire.

John 15:4-6

Abide in Me, and I in you. As the branch cannot bear fruit of itself, unless it abides in the vine, neither can you, unless you abide in Me. I am the vine, you are the branches. He who abides in Me, and I in him, bears much fruit; for without Me you can do nothing. If anyone does not abide in Me, he is cast out as a branch and is withered; and they gather them and throw them into the fire, and they are burned.

This word was spoken to believers, not unbelievers. Jesus was exhorting believers to abide in Him so that they would bear fruit. If anyone does not abide in the vine, *"he is cast out as a branch and is withered; and they gather them and throw them into the fire, and they are burned."* This runs parallel to the Parable of the Tares. It is difficult to distinguish between wheat and tares when they start growing. It is only at harvest time that the wheat stocks begin to bend over with the weight of the grain on them. The tares do not bend, for they do not produce any edible grain. Instead, they are like a weed and are subject to be burned.

Let's look closer at what will happen for those who are resurrected and get cast into a *"furnace of fire."* We should note that although there has been a separation made, this is **before** the Judgment Seat of Christ.

1 Corinthians 3:11-15

For no other foundation can anyone lay than that which is laid, which is Jesus Christ. Now if anyone builds on this foundation with gold, silver, precious stones, wood, hay, straw, each one's work will become clear; **for the Day will declare it**, *because it will be* **revealed by fire**; *and the* **fire will test each one's work, of what sort it is.** *If anyone's work which he has built on it endures, he will receive a reward. If anyone's work is burned, he will suffer loss; but he himself will be saved,* **yet so as through fire.**

This is a time of humility, remorse, testing and purification for those who are found not ready as the Judgment Seat approaches. In the next chapter we will look at what happens between the Resurrection and the Judgment Seat. I will suggest that specific end-time events will happen during this period. We'll endeavor to place some puzzle pieces together and see if they fit.

CHAPTER 13

FROM THE RESURRECTION TO THE JUDGMENT SEAT

How much time do you think there will be between the Resurrection and the Judgment Seat of Christ? Further on in Chapter 19, "How the Fall Feasts Could Be Fulfilled," I propose that the Resurrection will happen at the Feast of Trumpets, and the Judgment Seat of Christ will happen at the Day of Atonement. Remember, the feasts were instituted by God and celebrated by the people of God to reveal events that would be coming in the future. The spring feasts have all been fulfilled on the exact day of the feast, consecutively, within one spring. What a coincidence! This happened to the amazement of believers but has been unnoticed by many Jews, who continue to wait for their fulfillment.

We'll talk further about this, but I wanted to mention it because there are ten Days of Awe that separate these two fall feasts. Traditionally, this is a time of soul searching and deep repentance, knowing that it is a fearful thing to stand before the judgment that will happen at the Day of Atonement. Those who celebrate now are doing a dress rehearsal of what it will really be like for the people of God to experience the fear and trembling of standing before the living God.

I strongly suggest that there will be exactly ten days between the resurrection of the saints and Jesus coming on a white horse as the heavens open up. Let's consider what might make these days filled with awe!

We had mentioned that the wedding happens during this time (at the top of Mount Zion), and interestingly, the Jewish tradition was that the groom would take his bride to his chambers that he had prepared and consummate the marriage over a week's time. The couple would then come out of the bridal chambers and celebrate the wedding feast with family and friends. Whether the wedding and feast actually happen during this time is open for discussion, but this understanding is useful in our study.

In previous chapters, we have noted how we have been grafted into Israel by faith and the promises to Israel are also our promises. So, where Israel goes, we also go. With that understanding, we will look at Old Testament end-time prophetic words to Israel that have not yet been fulfilled concerning their resurrection, testing and restoration into the Kingdom. As we read these prophecies, I hope you let these scriptures reveal to you how these words might unfold. We will be making some conjecture in placing these puzzle pieces together, for how else will we know whether they fit? We are trying to solve a mystery. Remember?

Ezekiel 20:33-44

"[As] I live," says the LORD GOD, *"surely with a mighty hand, with an outstretched arm, and with fury poured out, I will rule over you.* **I will bring you out from the peoples and gather you out of the countries where you are scattered, with a mighty hand, with an outstretched arm, and with fury poured out.** *"And I will bring you into the wilderness of the peoples, and there I will plead My case with you face to face. "Just as I pleaded My case with your fathers in the wilderness of the land of Egypt, so I will plead My case with you,"* says the LORD GOD.

"I will make you pass under the rod, and I will bring you into the bond of the covenant; "I will purge the rebels from among you, and those who transgress against Me; I will bring them out of the country where they dwell, but they shall not enter the land of Israel. Then you will know that I [am] the LORD.

"As for you, O house of Israel," thus says the LORD GOD: "Go, serve every one of you his idols — and hereafter — if you will not obey Me; but profane My holy name no more with your gifts and your idols. **For on My holy mountain, on the mountain height of Israel," says the LORD GOD, "there all the house of Israel, all of them in the land, shall serve Me; there I will accept them, and there I will require your offerings and the firstfruits of your sacrifices, together with all your holy things.** I will accept you as a sweet aroma when I bring you out from the peoples and gather you out of the countries where you have been scattered; and I will be hallowed in you before the Gentiles. **Then you shall know that I [am] the LORD when I bring you into the land of Israel, into the country [for] which I raised My hand in an oath to give to your fathers. And there you shall remember your ways and all your doings with which you were defiled; and you shall loathe yourselves in your own sight because of all the evils that you have committed.** Then you shall know that I [am] the LORD, when I have dealt with you for My name's sake, not according to your wicked ways nor according to your corrupt doings, O house of Israel," says the LORD GOD.

This prophecy will be fulfilled and we will experience it fully as the people of God. It reveals the gathering (Resurrection) of all God's people, it reveals the deep chastening of the Lord as rebellion and sins are exposed, and it reveals the promised inheritance of the land to those found faithful. For those not selected as the Bride (on the mountaintop), it will be a time of fear and trembling, a deep shaking. The fear of the Lord will be known by those approaching the Judgment Seat of Christ. It will be 10 Days of Awe.

We should note these events happen *"on My holy mountain, on the mountain height of Israel."* The mountain of the Lord or Mount Zion have been elusive to me, since sometimes they seem to refer to a real mountain and sometimes to a cosmic spiritual presence that may or may not be perceived with the naked eye. This mountain will be massive, since it will contain all the righteous throughout time. It would be rooted on the earth but could extend far into the heavens, most probably surrounded by clouds at the top.

The righteous, in their resurrected state, could not only be *on* it, but also *in* it. Remember how Jesus, in His resurrected state, could walk through walls and was not constrained by physical barriers and yet could communicate and eat.

During Moses time, there was a distinction between the top of the mountain and the bottom of the mountain:

Exodus 19:13-20

*"Not a hand shall touch him, but he shall surely be stoned or shot with an arrow; whether man or beast, he shall not live. **When the trumpet sounds long, they shall come near the mountain."***

So Moses went down from the mountain to the people and sanctified the people, and they washed their clothes. And he said to the people, "Be ready for the third day; do not come near your wives."

*Then it came to pass on the third day, in the morning, that there were thunderings and lightnings, and a thick cloud on the mountain; and the sound of the trumpet was very loud, so that all the people who were in the camp trembled. **And Moses brought the people out of the camp to meet with God, and they stood at the foot of the mountain.** Now Mount Sinai was completely in smoke, because the LORD descended upon it in fire. Its smoke ascended like the smoke of a* *furnace, and the whole mountain quaked greatly. And when the blast of the trumpet sounded long and became louder and louder, Moses spoke, and God answered him by voice.* **Then the LORD came down upon Mount Sinai, on the top of the mountain. And the LORD called Moses to the top of the mountain, and Moses went up.**

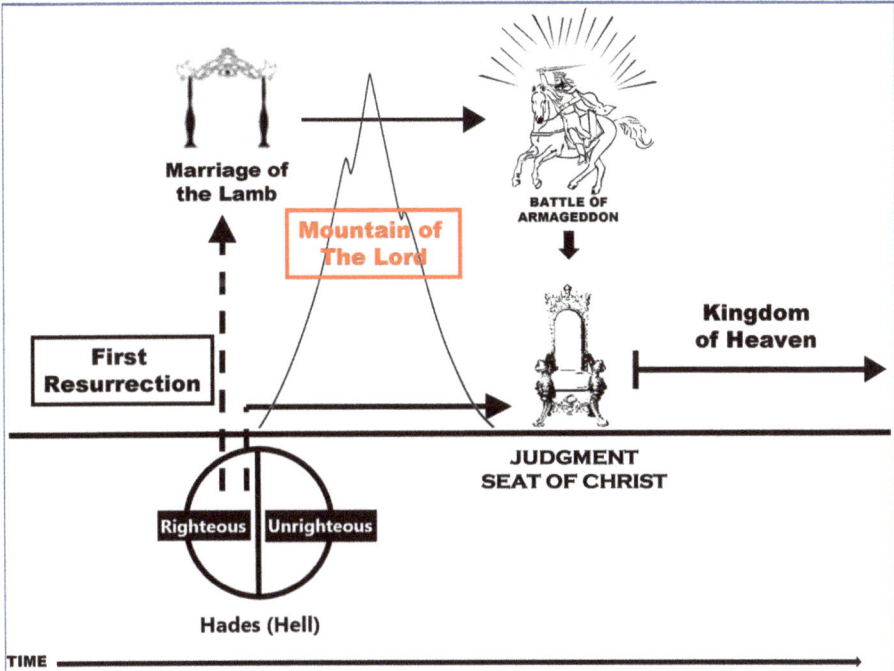

One important point to note is: *"When the trumpet sounds long, they shall come near the mountain."* This parallels with the coming of the Lord and the saints resurrecting at the blowing of the trumpet. God's glory was on the top of the mountain, and most of the people were at the foot of it. The wicked among the congregation at the foot of the mountain were revealed through their idolatry and rebellion and were judged severely. I would suggest that the Bride will be on top of the *"holy mountain,"* while others will be at its base on the Earth.

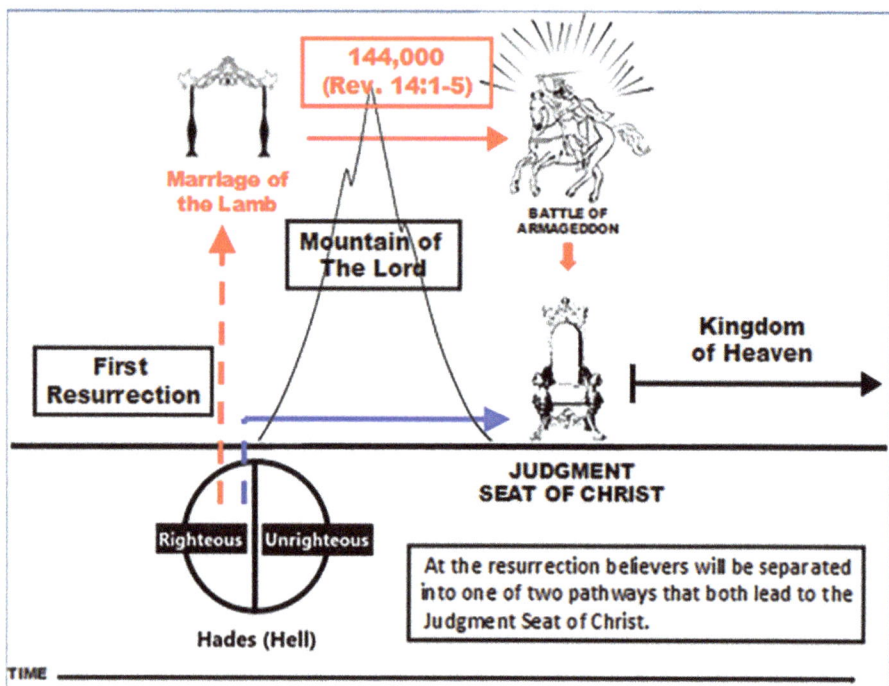

Matthew 24:37-44

But as the days of Noah were, so also will the coming of the Son of Man be. For as in the days before the flood, they were eating and drinking, marrying and giving in marriage, until the day that Noah entered the ark, and did not know until the flood came and took them all away, so also will the coming of the Son of Man be. Then two men will be in the field: one will be taken and the other left. Two women will be grinding at the mill: one will be taken and the other left. Watch therefore, for you do not know what hour your Lord is coming. But know this, that if the master of the house had known what hour the thief would come, he would have watched and not allowed his house to be broken into. Therefore you also be ready, for the Son of Man is coming at an hour you do not expect.

Let me give an explanation of this scripture in light of the separation that will happen to believers at the First Resurrection and also with the idea of the mountain of the Lord. Remember where Jesus was when He was telling this story and who He was talking to. He was talking to the righteous and was on the actual land where the righteous will land at the Resurrection. The *"coming of the Son of Man"* will be like the days of Noah. Those who were ready were in the ark and would rise when the flood came.

Genesis 7:19-20

And the waters prevailed exceedingly on the earth, and all the high hills under the whole heaven were covered. The waters prevailed fifteen cubits upward, and the mountains were covered.

At the Resurrection, *"one will be taken"* (ascending to the mountaintop) *"and the other left"* (staying on the ground or at the base of the mountain). This exhortation is for the righteous to be ready when the Lord comes. Those who are not ready will be like someone who has something stolen from them. What was stolen? The inheritance of being the Bride was taken away, like the virgins without their oil. Those virgins were not ready and could not arise and enter into the wedding feast.

What is the "Furnace of Fire?" I want to revisit this phrase, *"furnace of fire,"* which is found in the Parable of the Dragnet and the Parable of the Tares. There are many references throughout the Scriptures that speak of a purifying fire that is to come upon Israel, and they have not yet been fulfilled.

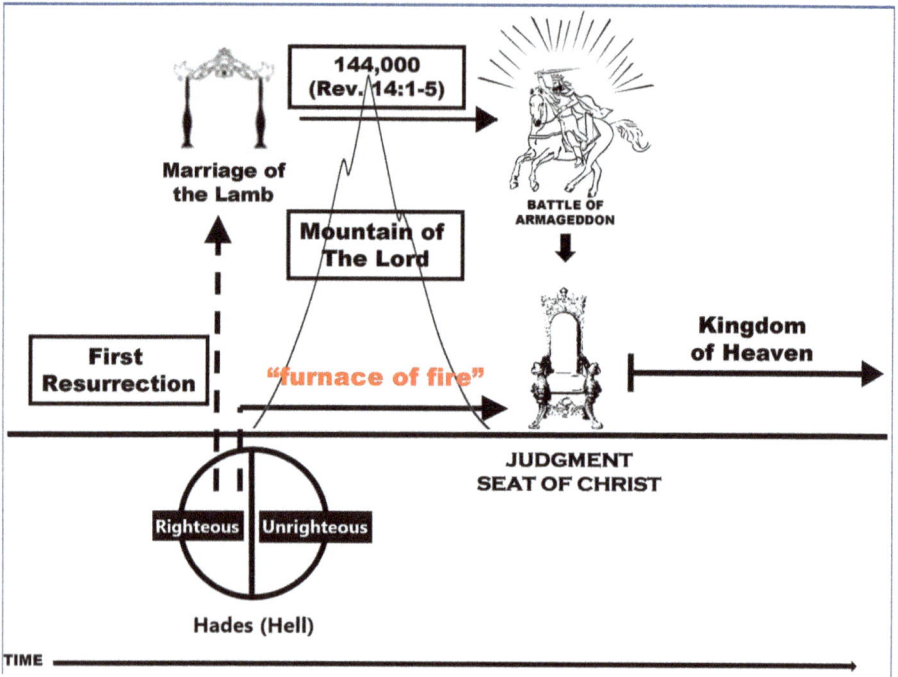

Deuteronomy 32:22

*For a **fire** is kindled in My anger,*
And shall burn to the lowest hell;
It shall consume the earth with her increase,
*And set on **fire** the **foundations of the mountains**.*

Malachi 3:2-3

*But who **can endure the day of His coming?***
And who can stand when He appears?
*For He is like **a refiner's fire***
And like launderers' soap.
He will sit as a refiner and a purifier of silver;
He will purify the sons of Levi,
And purge them as gold and silver,

That they may offer to the LORD
An offering in righteousness.

We should note that a furnace is used to make or perfect something so as to make it more valuable. This is different from a fire which destroys. This fire will not destroy the spirit of the righteous because the spirit is eternal. In the same way, gold is not destroyed when it is refined; only the impurities in it are burned up. The *furnace of fire* is another example of the Hell (*Gehenna*) fire that Jesus warned believers of.

Now, I want to show you scriptures that reveal a correlation between the time that Israel was in Egypt and the *furnace of fire* which will come at the end of this age:

Deuteronomy 4:20, KJV

But the LORD hath taken you, and brought you forth out of **the iron furnace***, even out of* **Egypt***, to be unto him a people of inheritance, as ye are this day.*

1 Kings 8:51, KJV

For they be thy people, and thine inheritance, which thou broughtest forth out of **Egypt***, from the midst of the* **furnace of iron:**

Jeremiah 11:3-5

And say to them, "Thus says the LORD God of Israel: 'Cursed is the man who does not obey the words of this covenant which I commanded your fathers in the day I brought them out of the land **of Egypt***, from* **the iron furnace***, saying, "Obey My voice, and do according to all that I command you; so shall you be My people, and I will be your God," that I may establish the oath which I have sworn to your fathers, to give them "a land flowing with milk and honey," as it is this day.'" And I answered and said, "So be it, LORD."*

Ezekiel 20:36-37

> *"Just as I pleaded My case with your fathers in the wilderness of the land of Egypt, so I will plead My case with you," says the* LORD God. *"I will make you pass under the rod, and I will bring you into the bond of the covenant."*

There is a very important point in this scripture. The coming fire on Israel will be like what happened to Israel in Egypt. What do we remember about what happened in Egypt? The ten plagues, which included turning the water of the Nile River into blood, frogs, lice, flies, animals dying, boils, thunder and hail, locusts, darkness and the firstborns dying. There is a very similar event, the Bowl Judgments, that will happen at the end of this age, which will happen when the righteous are resurrected onto the land of Israel.

Revelation 16:1-21

> *Then I heard a loud voice from the temple saying to the seven angels, "Go and pour out the bowls of the wrath of God on the earth."*
> *So the first went and poured out his bowl upon the earth, and a foul and loathsome sore came upon the men who had the mark of the beast and those who worshiped his image.*
> *Then the second angel poured out his bowl on the sea, and it became blood as of a dead man; and every living creature in the sea died.*
> *Then the third angel poured out his bowl on the rivers and springs of water, and they became blood. And I heard the angel of the waters saying:*
>
> *"You are righteous, O Lord,*
> *The One who is and who was and who is to be,*
> *Because You have judged these things.*
> *For they have shed the blood of saints and prophets,*
> *And You have given them blood to drink.*
> *For it is their just due."*

And I heard another from the altar saying, "Even so, Lord God Almighty, true and righteous are Your judgments."

Then the fourth angel poured out his bowl on the sun, and power was given to him to scorch men with fire. And men were scorched with great heat, and they blasphemed the name of God who has power over these plagues; and they did not repent and give Him glory.

Then the fifth angel poured out his bowl on the throne of the beast, and his kingdom became full of darkness; and they gnawed their tongues because of the pain. They blasphemed the God of heaven because of their pains and their sores, and did not repent of their deeds.

Then the sixth angel poured out his bowl on the great river Euphrates, and its water was dried up, so that the way of the kings from the east might be prepared. And I saw three unclean spirits like frogs coming out of the mouth of the dragon, out of the mouth of the beast, and out of the mouth of the false prophet. For they are spirits of demons, performing signs, which go out to the kings of the earth and of the whole world, to gather them to the battle of that great day of God Almighty.

"Behold, I am coming as a thief. Blessed is he who watches, and keeps his garments, lest he walk naked and they see his shame."

And they gathered them together to the place called in Hebrew, Armageddon.

Then the seventh angel poured out his bowl into the air, and a loud voice came out of the temple of heaven, from the throne, saying, "It is done!" And there were noises and thunderings and lightnings; and there was a great earthquake, such a mighty and great earthquake as had not occurred since men were on the earth. Now the great city was divided into three parts, and the cities of the nations fell. And great Babylon was remembered before God, to give her the cup of the wine of the fierceness of His wrath. Then every island fled away, and the mountains were not found. And great hail from heaven fell upon men, each hailstone about the weight of a talent. Men blasphemed God because of the plague of the hail, since that plague was exceedingly great.

These epic events (the Bowl Judgments) will happen just before the Battle of Armageddon and after the Resurrection. The saints will be resurrected before the Bowl Judgments, because it says, *"They blasphemed the name of God who has power over these plagues; and they did not repent and give Him glory."* I believe that these judgments will be seen by the people of God who will be on the Earth in the same way that Israel, while in Goshen, witnessed God's tremendous wrath upon Egypt.

We will also see the power and strength of the Beast and the kings of the world who will amass, intent upon destroying the people of God. In the same way that Pharaoh and his army descended upon the Israelites to slaughter them when their backs were to the sea, so the monstrous end-time horde of men and demons will move fiercely to crush the people of God at Armageddon. In the same way, Jesus will come back with great power, to save His people at the last moment and crush all of His enemies. It will be epic!

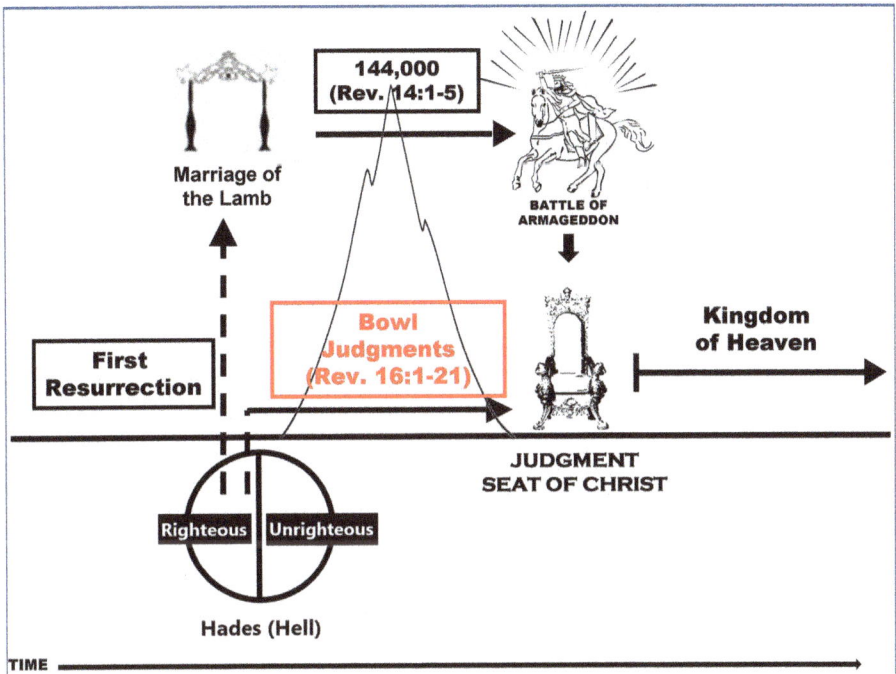

I know that this next scripture is a long one, but I can't tell it any better than Jeremiah did:

Jeremiah 30:3-11

"For behold, the days are coming," says the LORD, "that I will bring back from captivity My people Israel and Judah," says the LORD. **"And I will cause them to return to the land that I gave to their fathers, and they shall possess it."**
Now these are the words that the LORD spoke concerning Israel and Judah.
"For thus says the LORD:
'We have heard a voice of trembling,
Of fear, and not of peace.
Ask now, and see,

111

Whether a man is ever in labor with child?
So why do I see every man with his hands on his loins
Like a woman in labor,
And all faces turned pale?
Alas! For that day is great,
So that none is like it;
And it is the time of Jacob's trouble,
But he shall be saved out of it.

'For it shall come to pass in that day,'
Says the LORD of hosts,
'That I will break his yoke from your neck,
And will burst your bonds;
Foreigners shall no more enslave them.
But they shall serve the LORD their God,
And David their king,
Whom I will raise up for them.'
'Therefore do not fear, O My servant Jacob,' says the LORD,
'Nor be dismayed, O Israel;
For behold, I will save you from afar,
And your seed from the land of their captivity.
Jacob shall return, have rest and be quiet,
And no one shall make him afraid.
'For I am with you,' says the LORD, 'to save you;
Though I make a full end of all nations where I have scattered you,
Yet I will not make a complete end of you.
But I will correct you in justice,
And will not let you go altogether unpunished.'

This prophetic scripture tells what will happen after the resurrection of Israel onto the Earth. It will be a time of travailing, of anguish, a time for a nation to mourn, a time to conquer the enemies of Israel, a time of restoration and a time to dwell on the land in peace. All those who call on the name of the Lord will be saved, and surely *"all of Israel will be saved"* at the last hour before the next age.

Now, let's take a brief overview of what will happen before the First Resurrection. We see that there will be seven seal judgments released on the Earth, followed by seven trumpet judgments, which will bring with them great calamity. After this, the Beast will arise onto the Earth and be given a fierce authority for forty-two months.

Revelation 13:7 and 10

It was granted to him [the Beast] *to make war with the saints and to overcome them. And authority was given him over every tribe, tongue, and nation.*

He who leads into captivity shall go into captivity; he who kills with the sword must be killed with the sword. Here is the patience and the faith of the saints.

Revelation 13:15-17

He [the Beast] *was granted power to give breath to the image of the beast, that the image of the beast should both speak and cause as many as would not worship the image of the beast to be killed. He causes all, both small and great, rich and poor, free and slave, to receive a mark on their right hand or on their foreheads, and that no one may buy or sell except one who has the mark or the name of the beast, or the number of his name.*

Persecution will be poured out on the saints up until the Resurrection. It will be a time that saints will have to persevere, endure and overcome.

Revelation 14:14-16

Then I looked, and behold, a white cloud, and on the cloud sat One like the Son of Man, having on His head a golden crown, and in His hand a sharp sickle. And another angel came out of the temple, crying with a loud voice to Him who sat on the cloud, "Thrust in Your sickle and reap, for the time has come for You to reap, for the harvest of the earth is ripe." So He who sat on the cloud thrust in His sickle on the earth, and the earth was reaped.

This is the First Resurrection.

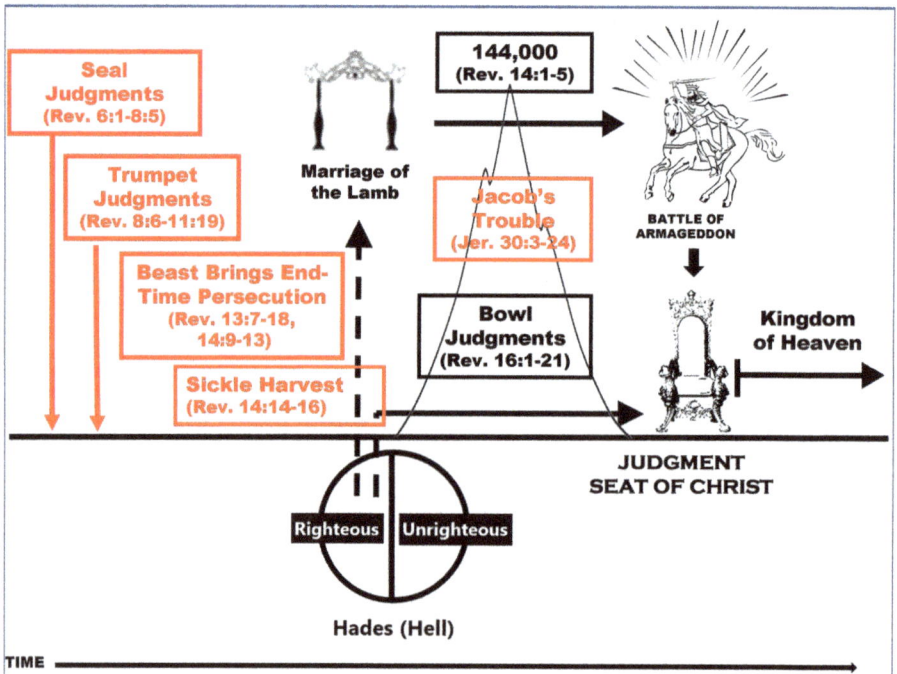

CHAPTER 14

THE JUDGMENT SEAT OF CHRIST

We will now take a look at the Judgment Seat of Christ and how various parables illustrate this event.

Romans 14:10-12

*But why do you judge your brother? Or why do you show contempt for your brother? For we shall all stand before **the judgment seat of Christ**. For it is written:*

"As I live, says the Lord,
Every knee shall bow to Me,
And every tongue shall confess to God."

So then each of us shall give account of himself to God.

2 Corinthians 5:10

*For we must all appear before **the judgment seat of Christ**, that each one may receive the things done in the body, according to what he has done, whether good or bad.*

I mentioned earlier in the book that only believers will be judged at the Judgment Seat of Christ, those who have come forth from the First Resurrection. When the Judgment Seat will actually take place is hidden to most, so we will look for some clues to verify my hunch about the timing of it.

Revelation 20:4

*And I saw **thrones**, and they sat on them, and judgment was committed to them. Then I saw the souls of those who had been beheaded for their witness to Jesus and for the word of God, who had not worshiped the beast or his image, and had not received his mark on their foreheads or on their hands. And they lived and reigned with Christ for a thousand years.*

In particular, let's look at **"thrones"** to see what we can find that would shed more light on this event. Shouldn't there be just one throne?

Matthew 19:28

*So Jesus said to them, "Assuredly I say to you, that in the regeneration, **when the Son of Man sits on the throne of His glory**, you who have followed Me will also sit **on twelve thrones**, judging the twelve tribes of Israel."*

"In [or at] the "regeneration," could also be translated as "when the world is made new," "in the new age," or "at the renewal of all things." The disciples *"who have followed [Him]"* will sit with Him to judge the twelve tribes of Israel. There will also be another throne that will be present. See if you can recognize clues to indicate that this is the Judgment Seat of Christ at the end of this age.

Daniel 7:9-14

*I watched till **thrones** were put in place,*
And the Ancient of Days was seated;

116

His garment was white as snow,
And the hair of His head was like pure wool.
His throne *was a fiery flame,*
Its wheels a burning fire;
A fiery stream issued
And came forth from before Him.
A thousand thousands ministered to Him;
Ten thousand times ten thousand stood before Him.
The court was seated,
And the books were opened.

I watched then because of the sound of the pompous words which the horn was speaking; I watched till the beast was slain, and its body destroyed and given to the burning flame. As for the rest of the beasts, they had their dominion taken away, yet their lives were prolonged for a season and a time.
"I was watching in the night visions,
And behold, One like the Son of Man,
Coming with the clouds of heaven!
He came to the Ancient of Days,
And they brought Him near before Him.
Then to Him was given dominion and glory and a kingdom,
That all peoples, nations, and languages should serve Him.
His dominion is an everlasting dominion,
Which shall not pass away,
And His kingdom the one
Which shall not be destroyed.

So, we see that the Father, the Ancient of Days, will be sitting on His throne among other thrones. He will give authority to the Son of Man to rule over a Kingdom which shall not pass away.

How can we verify that this is at the beginning of the Kingdom of Heaven?

> *I watched till the beast was slain, and its body destroyed and given to the burning flame. As for the rest of the beasts, they had their dominion taken away, yet their lives were prolonged for a season and a time.*

If we remember, in Revelation 19:20 through Revelation 20:3, the Beast and the False Prophet will be thrown into the Lake of Fire, and Satan will be bound for a thousand years. This will happen at the end of this age and the start of the Kingdom of Heaven. Satan's life will be *"prolonged for a season,"* for a thousand years to be exact.

Now let's look at parables that reveal the Judgment Seat of Christ.

CHAPTER 15

THE PARABLE OF
THE TALENTS

Matthew 25:14-30

For **the kingdom of heaven is like** *a man traveling to a far country,
who called his own servants and delivered his goods to them. And to
one he gave five talents, to another two, and to another one, to each
according to his own ability; and immediately he went on a journey.
Then he who had received the five talents went and traded with them,
and made another five talents. And likewise he who had received two
gained two more also. But he who had received one went and dug in the
ground, and hid his lord's money. After a long time the lord of those
servants came and settled accounts with them.*

*So he who had received five talents came and brought five other talents,
saying, "Lord, you delivered to me five talents; look, I have gained five
more talents besides them." His lord said to him, "Well done, good and
faithful servant; you were faithful over a few things, I will make you
ruler over many things. Enter into the joy of your lord." He also who
had received two talents came and said, "Lord, you delivered to me
two talents; look, I have gained two more besides them." His lord said
to him, "Well done, good and faithful servant; you have been faithful
over a few things, I will make you ruler over many things. Enter into
the joy of your lord."*

119

Then he who had received the one talent came and said, "Lord, I knew you to be a hard man, reaping where you have not sown, and gathering where you have not scattered seed. And I was afraid, and went and hid your talent in the ground. Look, there you have what is yours." But his lord answered and said to him, "You wicked and lazy servant, you knew that I reap where I have not sown, and gather where I have not scattered seed. So you ought to have deposited my money with the bankers, and at my coming I would have received back my own with interest. Therefore take the talent from him, and give it to him who has ten talents. For to everyone who has, more will be given, and he will have abundance; but from him who does not have, even what he has will be taken away. And cast the unprofitable servant into the outer darkness. There will be weeping and gnashing of teeth."

Many times, the servants in the parables are misinterpreted to be both believers and unbelievers, since the punishment seems to be eternal wrath (the Lake of Fire), but it is not. So, we have:

*The kingdom of heaven is like a man traveling to a far country, who called **his own servants** and delivered **his goods** to them. And to one he gave five talents, to another two, and to another one, to each according to his own ability; and immediately **he went on a journey.***

God calls us to Himself and gives us talents. A talent is something of value you can weigh or measure. The Holy Spirit has immeasurable worth.

*After a **long time,** the lord of those servants **came and settled accounts** with them.*

Jesus is coming back and will settle accounts at the Judgment Seat of Christ.

*So he who had received five talents came and brought five other talents, saying, "Lord, you delivered to me five talents; look, I have gained five more talents besides them." His lord said to him, "Well done, **good and faithful servant; you were faithful over a few things, I will make you ruler over many things.** Enter into the joy of your lord."*

Our reward will be becoming *"ruler over many things."* This means ruling and reigning with Christ for a thousand years. This is the inheritance of the Kingdom.

The corresponding parable, as recorded in Luke, is even clearer:

Luke 19:17

And he said to him, "Well done, good servant; because you were faithful in a very little, have authority over ten cities."

Authority over cities will be given at the Judgment Seat of Christ as a reward for good works done. The same sequence is seen with two talents:

Then he who had received the one talent came and said, "Lord, I knew you to be a hard man, reaping where you have not sown, and gathering where you have not scattered seed. And I was afraid, and went and hid your talent in the ground. Look, there you have what is yours."

This servant was afraid. There is a difference between being afraid and having a fear of the Lord. When we are afraid and we know the

Lord, we usually are sinning, because we end up accusing God of being someone that He is not. If you are afraid of God, you are accusing Him of being mean, of not being merciful, of not being compassionate.

"So you ought to have deposited my money with the bankers, and at my coming I would have received back my own with interest. Therefore take the talent from him, and give it to him who has ten talents. For to everyone who has, more will be given, and he will have abundance; but from him who does not have, even what he has will be taken away."

We mentioned the Outer Darkness before, and this is another description of what Hell (*Gehenna*) is. This is a place of punishment for believers who are awaiting the final Great White Judgment, after which time there will be no more suffering.

Let's put this in perspective: Jesus was revealing to us how He will judge. These are His words. He is not mean spirited. He was being direct in showing us how He will judge. Do not be afraid and run from Him. Bow and repent, if you need to, and then press into God. Knowing the fear of the Lord is good, for it makes us ready!

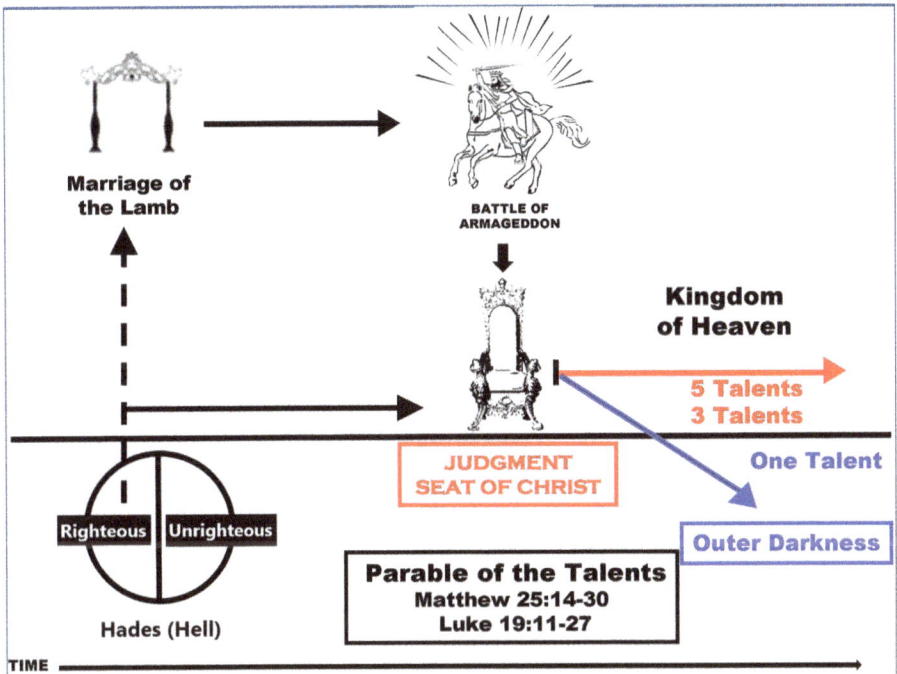

Marriage of
the Lamb

BATTLE OF
ARMAGEDDON

Kingdom
of Heaven

5 Talents
3 Talents

JUDGMENT
SEAT OF CHRIST

One Talent

Outer Darkness

Righteous | Unrighteous

Hades (Hell)

Parable of the Talents
Matthew 25:14-30
Luke 19:11-27

TIME

CHAPTER 16

THE PARABLE OF THE UNFORGIVING SERVANT

We have gone over the interpretation of this parable in an earlier chapter, but I want to add some further points. As we can see, this parable illustrates the salvation of the believer, the Judgment Seat of Christ and the consequence of Hell (*Gehenna*).

Jesus told this parable on unforgiveness after the following exchange with Peter:

Matthew 18:15-18 and 21-22

Moreover if your brother sins against you, go and tell him his fault between you and him alone. If he hears you, you have gained your brother. But if he will not hear, take with you one or two more, that "by the mouth of two or three witnesses every word may be established." And if he refuses to hear them, tell it to the church. But if he refuses even to hear the church, let him be to you like a heathen and a tax collector. **Assuredly, I say to you, whatever you bind on earth will be bound in heaven, and whatever you loose on earth will be loosed in heaven.**

Then Peter came to Him and said, "Lord, how often shall my brother sin against me, and I forgive him? Up to seven times?"

Jesus said to him, "I do not say to you, up to seven times, but up to seventy times seven."

These instructions on forgiveness illustrate to us how we loose and bind. An expanded verse on how to loose and bind might be helpful in our study:

Matthew 16:19

*And I will give you the **keys of the kingdom of heaven**, and whatever you bind on earth will be bound in heaven, and whatever you loose on earth will be loosed in heaven.*

Jesus was telling Peter that He was going to give him *"the keys to the Kingdom of Heaven."* Our first thought should be to make a copy of those keys in case we lose them. Keys give one the authority to go into a place, in this case, specifically, into the Kingdom of Heaven.

The Parable of the Unforgiving Servant solves what it means to loose and bind. If you bind man's sins on Earth, your sins will be bound in Heaven, and if you loose (forgive) man's sins on Earth, your sins will be loosed (forgiven). That's an important key, and you don't want to lose it.

Now, what good is a key if you don't use it? Do you have anyone you need to forgive or someone you have made a judgment against?

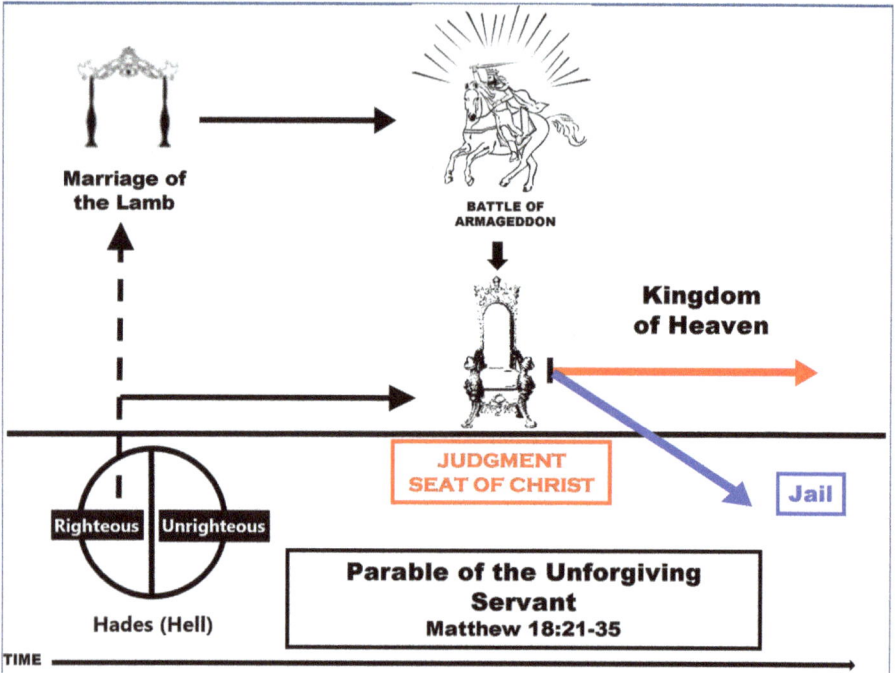

Marriage of
the Lamb

BATTLE OF
ARMAGEDDON

Kingdom
of Heaven

JUDGMENT
SEAT OF CHRIST

Jail

Righteous | Unrighteous

Hades (Hell)

**Parable of the Unforgiving
Servant**
Matthew 18:21-35

TIME

CHAPTER 17

THE PARABLE OF THE WEDDING FEAST

Matthew 22:1-14

And Jesus answered and spoke to them again by parables and said: "**The kingdom of heaven is like** *a certain king who arranged a marriage for his son, and sent out his servants to call those who were invited to the wedding; and they were not willing to come. Again, he sent out other servants, saying, 'Tell those who are invited, "See, I have prepared my dinner; my oxen and fatted cattle are killed, and all things are ready. Come to the wedding."' But they made light of it and went their ways, one to his own farm, another to his business. And the rest seized his servants, treated them spitefully, and killed them. But when the king heard about it, he was furious. And he sent out his armies, destroyed those murderers, and burned up their city. Then he said to his servants, 'The wedding is ready, but those who were invited were not worthy. Therefore go into the highways, and as many as you find, invite to the wedding.' So those servants went out into the highways and gathered together all whom they found, both bad and good. And the wedding hall was filled with guests.*

"*But when the king came in to see the guests, he saw a man there who did not have on a wedding garment. So he said to him, 'Friend, how did you come in here without a wedding garment?' And he was speechless.*

Then the king said to the servants, 'Bind him hand and foot, take him away, and cast him into outer darkness; there will be weeping and gnashing of teeth.'
"For many are called, but few are chosen."

We could spend a lot of time on this, but I just want to make a few points. The Kingdom of Heaven is like a king who arranged a marriage for his son. He sent out invitations to many he knew, but they all refused him. They even killed his messengers, which made him so angry that he destroyed their city and its inhabitants.

The king then told his servants to go to the highways and byways and invite all they encountered to this wedding. The Wedding is the marriage of Christ with His Bride. Those given the first invitation were the Jews, but they refused to come. They even killed the prophets, and the result was that God brought judgment upon them through other nations. In 70 AD, the city of Jerusalem was burned down and plowed over. The invitation to the Wedding was now opened up to the Gentiles.

Let's focus on this:

But when the king came in to see the guests, he saw a man there who did not have on a wedding garment. So he said to him, "Friend, how did you come in here without a wedding garment?" And he was speechless. Then the king said to the servants, "Bind him hand and foot, take him away, and cast him into outer darkness; there will be weeping and gnashing of teeth."

I would suggest that the man not wearing a wedding garment was not an unbeliever, since only Christians would be at this Wedding. Only Christians would have been resurrected to this place. The Judgment of Outer Darkness is made at the Judgment Seat of Christ, and it is for believers who are found lacking.

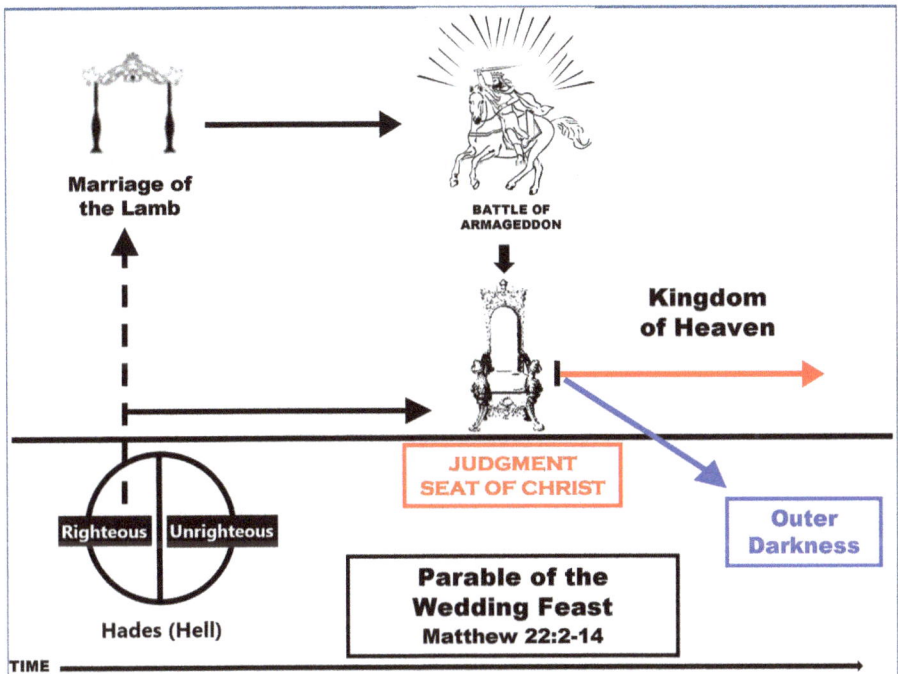

Where else do we find Jesus exhorting believers to be properly clothed?

Revelation 3:3-5

Remember therefore how you have received and heard; hold fast and repent. Therefore if you will not watch, I will come upon you as a thief, and you will not know what hour I will come upon you. You have a few names even in Sardis who have not defiled their garments; and they shall walk with Me in white, for they are worthy. He who overcomes shall be clothed in white garments, and I will not blot out his name from the Book of Life; but I will confess his name before My Father and before His angels.

Jesus was telling the church in Sardis that some had not defiled their garments and would walk with Him in white. This also means that some need to hold fast and repent or else they will not walk with Jesus, because they will be found unworthy. Instead of being with Him in the Kingdom, they will be in Outer Darkness.

I want to address the phrase, *"and I will not blot out his name from the Book of Life,"* since this seems like a believer could lose his salvation and end up in the Lake of Fire. I want to mention that there are several Books of Life. There is the Book of Life at the Great White Throne, and there is the Lamb's Book of Life at the Judgment Seat of Christ. These books determine who will **live** in the next age.

Here is a reference to the Lamb's Book of Life:

Revelation 21:27

But there shall by no means enter it anything that defiles, or causes an abomination or a lie, but only those who are written in the Lamb's Book of Life.

When we believe in Christ, our name is placed into both the Book of Life and the Lamb's Book of Life. Your name can be blotted out of the Lamb's Book of Life, but not out of the Book of Life. You can only have your name blotted out if it was placed there to begin with.

There are inheritances that we can lose, and by the time many realize this fact, it will be too late, and there will be weeping and gnashing of teeth. The time to repent is now!

Now, I want to go back to the end of the parable which speaks of the man who did not have on a wedding garment and was cast into Outer Darkness. That last verse reads as follows:

For many are called, but few are chosen.

Who are the *"called,"* and who are the *"chosen"*? The *called,* in this parable, seem to be those who are invited to the Wedding. There are certainly many who have been called. The man without the wedding garments was **not** *"chosen"* precisely because he didn't have wedding garments on, although he could have had them on. This is similar to the virgins who did not have oil. They had access to oil, but did not avail themselves of it. God is not just selecting His elect by choosing them indiscriminately; He is choosing men and women based on the choices they themselves have made.

2 Timothy 2:20-21

> *But in a great house there are not only vessels of gold and silver, but also of wood and clay, some for honor and some for dishonor. Therefore if anyone cleanses himself from the latter, he will be a vessel for honor, sanctified and useful for the Master, prepared for every good work.*

CHAPTER 18

THE SON OF MAN
JUDGES THE NATIONS

Matthew 25:31-46

When the Son of Man comes in His glory, and all the holy angels with Him, then He will sit on the throne of His glory. All the nations will be gathered before Him, and He will separate them one from another, as a shepherd divides his sheep from the goats. And He will set the sheep on His right hand, but the goats on the left. Then the King will say to those on His right hand, "Come, you blessed of My Father, inherit the kingdom prepared for you from the foundation of the world: for I was hungry and you gave Me food; I was thirsty and you gave Me drink; I was a stranger and you took Me in; I was naked and you clothed Me; I was sick and you visited Me; I was in prison and you came to Me." Then the righteous will answer Him, saying, "Lord, when did we see You hungry and feed You, or thirsty and give You drink? When did we see You a stranger and take You in, or naked and clothe You? Or when did we see You sick, or in prison, and come to You?" And the King will answer and say to them, "Assuredly, I say to you, inasmuch as you did it to one of the least of these My brethren, you did it to Me." Then He will also say to those on the left hand, "Depart from Me, you cursed, into the everlasting fire prepared for the devil and his angels: for I was hungry and you gave Me no food; I was thirsty and you gave Me no drink; I was a stranger and you did not take Me in, naked and you did not clothe Me, sick and in prison and you did not visit Me."

Then they also will answer Him, saying, "Lord, when did we see You hungry or thirsty or a stranger or naked or sick or in prison, and did not minister to You?" Then He will answer them, saying, "Assuredly, I say to you, inasmuch as you did not do it to one of the least of these, you did not do it to Me." And these will go away into everlasting punishment, but the righteous into eternal life.

When the Son of Man comes in His glory, and all the holy angels with Him, then He will sit on the throne of His glory.

This shows the end of this age, when Jesus will come in power with His angels. This passage also describes Jesus sitting on His judgment seat, about to judge His people from every tribe and nation. His judgment will be based on what they have done and what they have left undone.

The sheep are those who fed those who were hungry, gave drink to those who were thirsty, clothed the naked and visited the sick and those in prison. Jesus said that when they did that to the least of His brethren, they did it to Him. The goats did not do any of these things. They lived for themselves and had no time for the poor.

To the sheep, He said, "**Inherit the kingdom** *prepared for you from the foundation of the world."* This is the inheritance of the Kingdom of Heaven. They also receive *"eternal life,"* which is the inheritance of all believers.

The goats were not judged because they stole from the poor or abused them, but because they neglected the needs of the poor. This is not a judgment of unbelievers but, rather, of the righteous who should have known better and done better.

Matthew 19:23-24

Then Jesus said to His disciples, "Assuredly, I say to you that it is hard for a rich man to enter the kingdom of heaven. And again I say to you, it is easier for a camel to go through the eye of a needle than for a rich man to enter the kingdom of God."

The goats will miss the Kingdom and are told, *"Depart from Me, you cursed, into the **everlasting** fire prepared for the devil and his angels,"* and are commanded, *"Go away into **everlasting** punishment."* Many believe that since the Lake of Fire is where unbelievers go to receive *"everlasting punishment"* and since the devil and his angels are cast into the Lake of Fire, then it would seem that the goats are unbelievers. But when you are trying to solve a mystery, you look beyond the obvious and search deeper.

We might ask, "Where are the devil and his angels at the time that judgment is made on the goats at the Judgment Seat of Christ?" I'll give you a hint: it's not the Lake of Fire. If you remember, the devil will be cast into the Bottomless Pit (see Revelation 20:1-3) at the beginning of the thousand-year reign, and the fallen angels will be in Hell *(Tartaroō)*. I would suggest that Hell *(Tartaroō)* and the Bottomless Pit are the same place. A deeper discussion on this topic is available on my website.[5]

2 Peter 2:4

For if God did not spare the angels who sinned, but cast them down to hell [Tartaroō] and delivered them into chains of darkness, to be reserved for judgment ...

This is the only time *Tartaroō* is used in the Scriptures. It is a specific place for fallen angels awaiting final judgment. The Bottomless Pit and Hell *(Tartaroō)* are **temporary** prisons for the Devil and his angels until they are released at the end of the thousand years. Then they will stand

5. www.thekingdomofheavenislike.com

134

before the Great White Throne Judgment and be sentenced to the Lake of Fire.

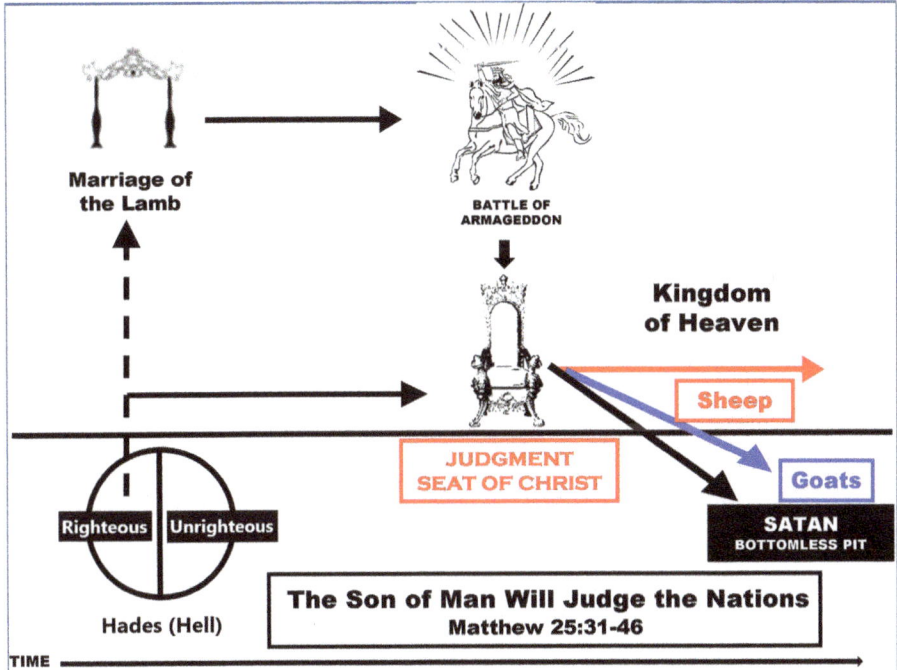

The Son of Man Will Judge the Nations
Matthew 25:31-46

Everlasting above seems to indicate infinity, but how can a thousand-year period that has a beginning and an end have infinity associated with it? The word translated *everlasting* in this scripture is the adjective *aiōnios* and comes from the noun *aion. Aion* can be translated as 1. eternity 2. the worlds, universe or 3. a period of time, an age. We will see that a better translation for *everlasting* would be "for the fullness of that age." The same thing is happening in the following scripture:

Exodus 21:5-6

> *But if the servant plainly says, "I love my master, my wife, and my children; I will not go out free," then his master shall bring him to the*

judges. He shall also bring him to the door, or to the doorpost, and his master shall pierce his ear with an awl; and he shall serve him **forever**.

The *forever* in this verse does not mean going on into infinity, but, rather, to the end of this man's life on earth. We find that there are many forevers in the Bible that have been completed or will be by the end of this world.

Now let's look at *aion*, the noun from which *aiōnios* is derived, to see how it can be used. *Aion* can be translated as "eternity," but can also be used to describe a particular age. For example:

Matthew 13:40

Therefore as the tares are gathered and burned in the fire, so it will be at the end of this **age** *[aion].*

This is talking about the end of this world (which does have an end).

Ephesians 2:7

That in **the ages** *[aion] to come He might show the exceeding riches of His grace in His kindness toward us in Christ Jesus.*

Philippians 4:20

Now to our God and Father be glory forever [aion] and ever [aion]. Amen.

Is the translation for *aion* as *forever* here indicating eternity? If so, it should read "from eternity and eternity," which doesn't make sense since you only need one eternity to go on to infinity. Intuitively, we know that "forever and ever" seems more eternal than just "forever." I want to suggest a reason for this. The translation should be "from age to age." The age after the thousand years will be an eternal age, since there will be no more death (see Revelation 21:4). Thus, we will give glory to God "through the ages" (including this one) into the age which is eternal.

I am taking time on this because it has had a great influence in how the church has interpreted this parable. Translators, for the most part, miss the thousand-year reign as being an age. They see eternity after our present age with folks going either to Heaven or the Lake of Fire. Thus, any eternal fire or punishment is seen as the Lake of Fire. When we understand the different ages, we can see that there can be a judgment or punishment in one of those ages without it going on for eternity.

This may be a good time to look at the attributes of Hell (*Gehenna*) that make it look like it is the Lake of Fire. In Matthew 18:8-9, Hell (*Gehenna*) is said to have an *"everlasting fire,"* which is what we saw the goats would experience. Mark 9:43-48 notes that the fire of Hell (*Gehenna*) will not be quenched and the worm will not die.

Remember, Hell (*Gehenna*) is a temporary place (or places) of punishment for believers until the Final Judgment. Let us look more closely at the "everlasting" descriptions of it. First, let's look closer at *"eternal fire"* to see what the Word of God has to say about it.

Jude 1:7

As Sodom and Gomorrah, and the cities around them in a similar manner to these, having given themselves over to sexual immorality and gone after strange flesh, are set forth as an example, suffering the vengeance of **eternal fire**.

Some archeologists say that they have found evidence of these cities, whose walls and footings look to have been destroyed by intense heat. It is obvious that Sodom and Gomorrah are not still burning today, so it didn't mean that the flames would burn without end forever, but, instead, that the effect of the fire would have an eternal result. Nothing would hinder that fire until it had its intended purpose fulfilled, which was the total destruction of physical buildings. In the same way, the punishment in Hell (*Gehenna*) will not be quenched by anyone in it, and the worms cannot be killed until every purpose of those worms has been achieved by God.

If we remember the Parable of the Unforgiving Servant, the master *"delivered him to the torturers until he should pay all that was due to him."* This debt was a specific amount that the master knew, no more and no less. In Matthew 5, when the man was going to the altar and realized that he needed to reconcile with his brother, the warning to him was that if he didn't reconcile, he would *"by no means get out of there* [prison] *till you have paid the last penny."* The judgment on that man would be for a specific amount and for a specific time.

Luke 12:47-49

And that servant who knew his master's will, and did not prepare himself or do according to his will, shall be beaten with many stripes. But he who did not know, yet committed things deserving of stripes, shall be beaten with few. For everyone to whom much is given, from him much will be required; and to whom much has been committed, of him they will ask the more. I came to send fire on the earth, and how I wish it were already kindled!

The point I want to make here is that the punishment for believers will be perfectly just and in accordance with one's failings. It will not go on indefinitely. The punishment will fit the crimes committed, for Jesus is a righteous judge. The *"everlasting punishment"* on the goats indicates that the punishment will not stop until it has completed the purpose for which it was rendered.

2 Peter 3:8, KJV

But, beloved, be not ignorant of this one thing, that one day is with the Lord as a thousand years, and a thousand years as one day.

For many, the hope will be that a thousand years will be like a day, but I am sure that a day of punishment could feel like a thousand years. An important point here is that those things that are not of Christ will be burned up. Remember, our spirit man is perfect. (It is no longer I who live but Christ in me.) It is eternal and holy in its nature. It is those carnal things attached to the soul and body that will be burned up (see Matthew 10:28).

When gold and silver are refined by fire to purify them, the impurities rise to the top and are skimmed off. The essence of the gold and silver is not changed, although it changes from solid to liquid. My friend Bryant Bullard once said, "You lose what you're not."

Now, as frightening as Hell fire seems, we must understand that this is the way of the Lord, and His ways are good and just. Nothing is ever done by Him to be mean or sadistic. What can we understand as to the nature and character of God by His instituting the place of Hell (*Gehenna*) for the righteous? Can we see that God is so steadfast in His faithfulness to us that if we become carnal and rebellious even after receiving the knowledge of the truth, He will perfect us through fire so that we might be with Him in eternity? The holy presence of the Lord will not be defiled by the presence of anything that is unclean, so the Lord, in His mercy, takes it upon Himself to restore us unto Himself. He remains faithful to His promise to us—even when we are unfaithful.

Malachi 3:3

He will sit as a refiner and a purifier of silver;
He will purify the sons of Levi,
And purge them as gold and silver,
That they may offer to the LORD
An offering in righteousness.

139

1 Peter 1:7

> *That the genuineness of your faith, being much more precious than gold that perishes, though it is tested by fire, may be found to praise, honor, and glory at the revelation of Jesus Christ,*

Could it be that the fire of Hell (*Gehenna*) is the only way God can restore a nation that has been rebellious and wayward? Could it be that this is how *"all of Israel will be saved"*?

Jeremiah 30:24

> *The fierce anger of the LORD will not return until He has done it,*
> *And until He has performed the intents of His heart.*
> *In the latter days you will consider it.*

Philippians 1:6

> *Being confident of this very thing, that He who has begun a good work in you will complete it until the day of Jesus Christ.*

CHAPTER 19

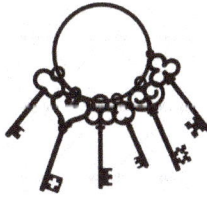

HOW THE FALL FEASTS COULD BE FULFILLED

I want to make just a brief overview of the feasts, since there are plenty of resources one can find on this topic.

God established different feasts that Israel was to celebrate over the year. These feasts were set on a lunar calendar, with each month beginning with a new moon. The feasts were foretelling of events that would happen in the future. The spring feasts were all fulfilled on the exact date that those feasts were celebrated, consecutively, in the same year.

- **Passover**—Jesus, our Passover lamb, was crucified at Passover.
- **Unleavened Bread**—Leaven is a symbol of sin, and Jesus had no sin. He was a perfect sacrifice. He was in the grave during this feast.
- **First Fruits**—Jesus resurrected on this feast day.
- **Pentecost**—This was when the Holy Spirit descended on believers with the evidence of tongues of fire.

The fall feasts have not been fulfilled yet, but it is expected by many that they will also be fulfilled on their appointed feast days. Some have thought that the fulfillment of each of the fall feasts will be separated by many years. It seems compelling, however, that the fall feasts will follow the pattern of the spring feasts, in that they were fulfilled in the same year, one right after the other. I have made some charts (of course) to illustrate where these fall feasts could be fulfilled.

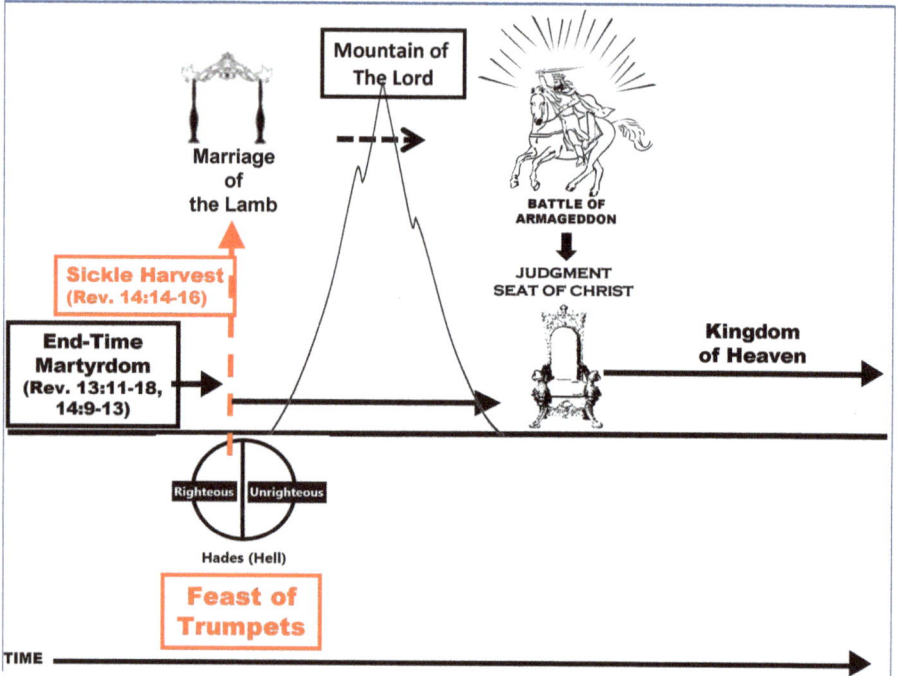

It is thought that the Feast of Trumpets will be fulfilled when the Church is resurrected and Christ comes back for His Bride. This feast includes the blowing of the trumpet, which is what will happen when the saints are taken up (see 1 Thessalonians 4:13-18 and 1 Corinthians 15:52).

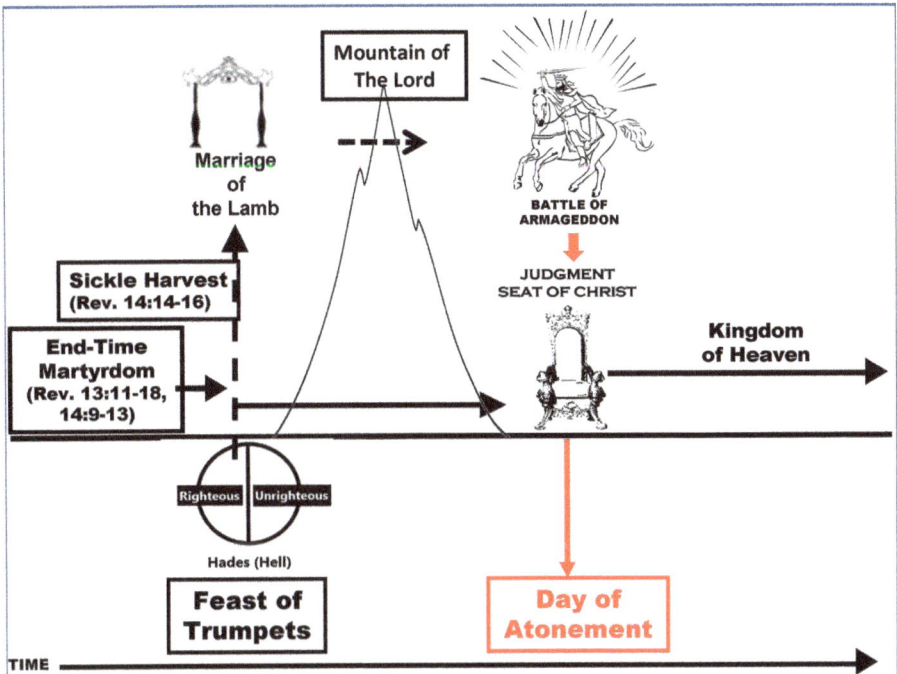

It is thought that the Day of Atonement will be fulfilled when Jesus comes to the Earth and judgment is made on the living. In ancient times, the Jewish High Priest would enter the Holy of Holies and make a sacrifice for the people on this day. This is a solemn and fearful day when the people of God recognize that each of them must stand before God and be judged.

143

The ten Days of Awe or the ten Days of Repentance are the days between the Feast of Trumpets and the Day of Atonement. Traditionally, this was a time of soul searching and deep repentance, knowing that it was a fearful thing to stand before the Judgment Seat coming at the Day of Atonement. Those who celebrate it now are only doing a dress rehearsal for what will come when a nation will be humbled and prostrate before the Lord. I believe that this will be the time of Jacob's Trouble and when the Bowl Judgments will be poured out.

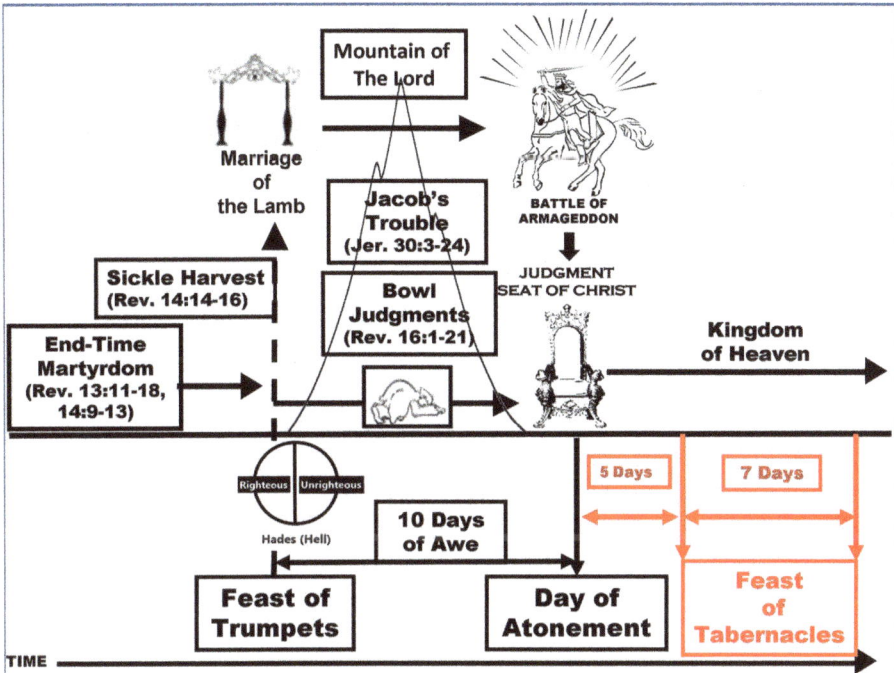

It should be easy at this point to see that the Feast of Tabernacles will be celebrated during the thousand-year reign of Christ. Those found faithful will be tabernacling with the Lord during the Kingdom of Heaven.

Zechariah 14:16-19

And it shall come to pass that everyone who is left of all the nations which came against Jerusalem shall go up from year to year to worship the King, the LORD of hosts, and to keep the Feast of Tabernacles. And it shall be that whichever of the families of the earth do not come up to Jerusalem to worship the King, the LORD of hosts, on them there will be no rain. If the family of Egypt will not come up and enter in, they shall have no rain; they shall receive the plague with which the LORD strikes the nations who do not come up to keep the Feast of Tabernacles.

This shall be the punishment of Egypt and the punishment of all the nations that do not come up to keep the Feast of Tabernacles.

This passage shows that the Feast of Tabernacles will be celebrated during the millennial reign, and there will be consequences for those who disregard this feast.

If we believe that the fall feasts will be fulfilled as the spring feasts were, we might note the dates of the coming Feast of Trumpets. Since the Jewish calendar is lunar based, it is different from our Gregorian calendar. Thus, each year has different dates for the feasts. The Jewish day begins and ends at sunset. So the feast begins at sundown of the first day noted and ends at the following sunset. We certainly should always be ready for Christ's coming, but remember, the feasts are a dress rehearsal for what is to come.

Historically, the Feast of Trumpets began when two witnesses saw the new moon and blew the trumpet. Weather conditions and alignment with the sun could prevent the moon from being seen over this two-day period. It was known as "the feast that no one knows the day or hour" of it's coming. In Matthew 24:36, Jesus said that no one knows the day and hour of His coming, except the Father. This may be a hint of when He will come. Certainly we know not the day or hour or year or century, but we are to be ready. This key understanding may be so obvious that it is hard to see.

Here are the corresponding dates for the Feast of Trumpets over the next few years:

2024—October 2-4
2025—September 22-24
2026—September 11-13

CHAPTER 20

THE SECOND DEATH

It would be instructive to look at when the Second Death will take place and note the distinction between the Second Death of the unbeliever and the believer. Let's begin with the unbeliever.

I have made a downward arrow in my charts which symbolizes death. When someone dies, they enter into Hades. This is a place where believers and unbelievers go to await their resurrection and final judgment. We'll look at Hades in more detail later, but I will mention here that there is a separation between the believers and unbelievers in Hades. The unbelievers will resurrect (the dotted line) at the end of the thousand-year reign of Christ and stand before the Great White Throne Judgment. Because of their unbelief, their names will not be in the Book of Life, and they will be cast into the Lake of Fire.

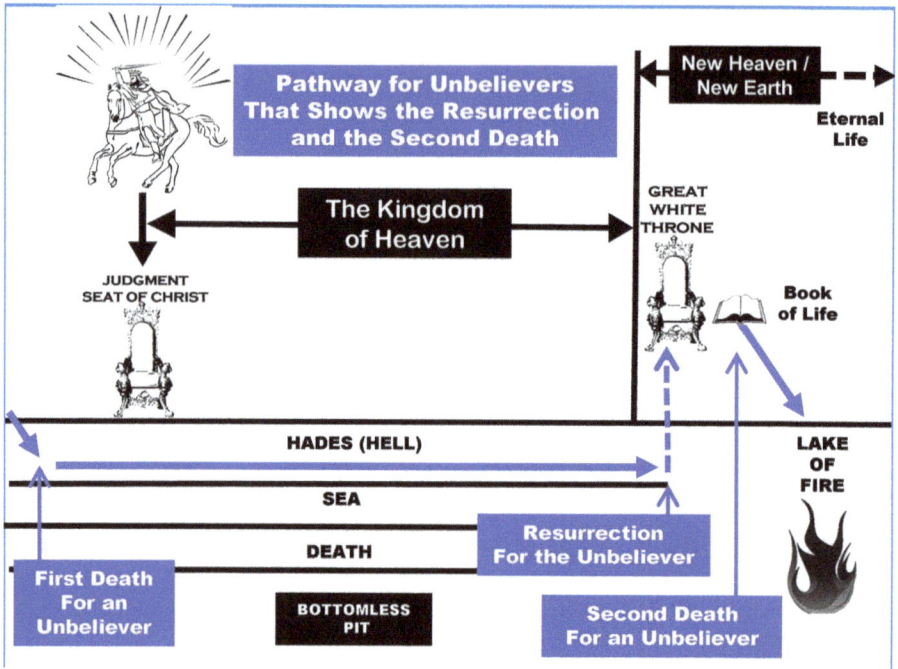

Revelation 20:14-15, KJV

And death and Hell were cast into the lake of fire. This is the second death [the lake of fire]. And whosoever was not found written in the book of life was cast into the lake of fire.

John 3:16-21

For God so loved the world that He gave His only begotten Son, that whoever believes in Him should not perish but have everlasting life. For God did not send His Son into the world to condemn the world, but that the world through Him might be saved. He who believes in Him is not condemned; but he who does not believe is condemned already, because he has not believed in the name of the only begotten Son of God. And this is the condemnation, that the light has come into the world, and men loved darkness rather than light, because their deeds were evil. For everyone practicing evil hates the light and does not come to the light, lest his deeds should be exposed. But he who does the truth comes to the light, that his deeds may be clearly seen, that they have been done in God.

God has allowed men and women to love, and this wonderful attribute requires us to have the ability to choose. Otherwise we would be mere robots, doing only what we were programmed to do. Since all can do good or bad, then we all fall short of being good. We are all condemned by the sin we have done.

The Lord is righteous and He requires justice for all sins committed. There will be no injustice, and that is why He came—so that men could be saved from sin. There is but one sacrifice for the forgiveness of man's sins that will bring us into right standing before God, and that is the sacrifice that Jesus made on the cross. Those who believe and repent of their sins will stand worthy before God.

Many will reject God and His offer. They will make their own rules, reject God's offer and love darkness. It is the heart of God that none perish but that all come to Him, but He has left the choice to us. There is a battle with Satan, who desires to kill, steal and destroy all that God loves. The enemy of God has sown an array of distractions, traps and seductions to keep men and women from God.

Acts 4:12

Nor is there salvation in any other, for there is no other name under heaven given among men by which we must be saved.

It is the eternal nature of God within those who believe that allows them to endure this fire and enter into eternal life. It is like gold that can withstand the fire and not be destroyed. Unbelievers will perish in the Lake of Fire. I believe that they will be consumed by fire and brought to nothing, just like the cities of Sodom and Gomorrah, because they have not received the eternal nature given to those who become born again. Many think that unbelievers will burn in torment forever. I don't think that reflects the true character of God, but we will look further into this at a later time.

John 3:5-6

Jesus answered, "Most assuredly, I say to you, unless one is born of water and the Spirit, he cannot enter the kingdom of God. That which is born of the flesh is flesh, and that which is born of the Spirit is spirit.

Either way, it is our duty and privilege to share the Good News that Jesus has made a way for all to receive eternal life by faith. For those who haven't yet trusted in Christ, I can only pray that you know the love that Jesus has for you and that you will come to trust in Him.

Romans 5:6-8

For when we were still without strength, in due time Christ died for the ungodly. For scarcely for a righteous man will one die; yet perhaps for a good man someone would even dare to die. But God demonstrates His own love toward us, in that while we were still sinners, Christ died for us.

Come to God, receive forgiveness for your sins, be baptized, and be filled with the Holy Spirit. Don't put this decision off. Your life depends upon it.

Now, I want to focus on the Second Death of the believers. I have again designated a downward arrow in my chart, which symbolizes our physical death into Hades. At the end of this age, the trumpet will sound, and the righteous will arise (which is shown as a dotted line). There will be a separation of believers at that point, which we have outlined earlier, but ultimately all believers stand before the Judgment Seat of Christ. There will be a judgment to determine whether one gets into the Kingdom of Heaven or not.

Two Pathways for Believers That Are Determined at the Judgment Seat of Christ

New Heaven / New Earth

Eternal Life

The Kingdom of Heaven

GREAT WHITE THRONE

JUDGMENT SEAT OF CHRIST

Book of Life

HADES

HADES (HELL)

LAKE OF FIRE

HELL (gehenna)

First Resurrection

SEA

First Death

Second Death for Carnal Believers

DEATH

BOTTOMLESS PIT

Second Resurrection for Carnal Believers

Those who are found faithful will enter into the Kingdom of Heaven and receive other rewards, as Christ sees fit. This is designated by the red line. After the thousand-year reign with Christ, they will find their name in the Book of Life and enter into eternal life (the New Heaven and New Earth), an inheritance that is received by faith.

Those believers who are judged unworthy to enter into the Kingdom of Heaven will receive a command from Jesus, *"Depart from me!"* This is the second death for the believer. These will follow the blue path, which will lead them down to Outer Darkness during the thousand-year reign. At the end of the thousand-year reign, they will resurrect for the second time (illustrated by the dotted lines) and stand before the Great White Throne Judgment. Their name will be in the Book of Life (because it was placed in there when they first believed), and they will receive their inheritance of eternal life (the New Heaven and New Earth).

We looked at the following scripture earlier:

Revelation 2:11

He who has an ear, let him hear what the Spirit says to the churches. **He who overcomes shall not be hurt by the second death.**

Again, those who do not overcome will be *"hurt"* by the Second Death. We should note that believers can suffer from the Second Death but not be destroyed or suffer in the Lake of Fire.

Revelation 20:4-6

*And I saw thrones and they sat on them. Then I saw the souls of those who had been beheaded for their witness to Jesus and the word of God, who had not worshipped the beast or his image and had not received his mark on their foreheads or on their hands. And they lived and reigned with Christ for a thousand years. But the rest of the dead did not live again until the thousand years were finished. This is the first resurrection. Blessed and holy is he who has part in the first resurrection. Over such the **second death** has no power, but they shall be priests of God and of Christ and shall reign with Him a thousand years.*

The First Resurrection will be the resurrection of the righteous. Those believers who are found to be *"blessed and holy "*will be *"priests of God and of Christ and shall reign with Him a thousand years."* For those who enter the Kingdom, the Second Death has no power. But the *"rest of the dead"* who were resurrected and were not found holy will suffer from the Second Death and *"not live again until the thousand years is finished."* At the end of the thousand years, they will live again by resurrecting and standing before the Great White Throne.

I want to bring insight to a scripture from the Parable of the Minas in Luke that corresponds to the Parable of the Talents in Matthew. These parables are similar, but one uses talents, and one uses minas to describe the treasure given to the three servants. We looked at how the master was angry with the servant, who returned the one talent with no gain. The result was the master cast that servant into Outer Darkness. Let's look at the added perspective in the judgment made on the servant with the one mina in Luke:

Luke 19:24-27

*And he said to those who stood by, "Take the mina from him, and give it to him who has ten minas." (But they said to him, "Master, he has ten minas.") "For I say to you, that to everyone who has will be given; and from him who does not have, even what he has will be taken away from him. But bring here those enemies of mine, who did not want me to reign over them, **and slay them before me."***

This is the Second Death at the Judgment Seat of Christ. It will be then that this servant is delivered into Outer Darkness. These two parables are revealing different components of the judgment to be visited upon believers who deny Christ by covering up their talents or *minas*.

So now we can better understand the following scriptures that exhort believers to live a holy life or suffer the consequences of death. It should be evident that the death being referenced is not a physical death. If you don't know what the Second Death is, then the impact of these core scriptures is diminished greatly.

Romans 8:12-13

*Therefore, brethren, we are debtors — not to the flesh, to live according to the flesh. For if you live according to the flesh you will **die**; but if by the Spirit you put to death the deeds of the body, you will live.*

James 2:17, 20 and 26

Thus also faith by itself, if it does not have works, is dead.

But do you want to know, O foolish man, that faith without works is dead?

*For as the body without the spirit is dead, so faith without works is **dead** also.*

Romans 6:16

*Do you not know that to whom you present yourselves slaves to obey, you are that one's slaves whom you obey, whether of sin leading to **death**, or of obedience leading to righteousness?*

Romans 8:6

*For to be carnally minded is **death**, but to be spiritually minded is life and peace.*

Matthew 10:39

He who finds his life will lose it, and he who loses his life for My sake will find it.

Matthew 10:28

And do not fear those who kill the body but cannot kill the soul. But rather fear Him who is able to destroy both soul and body in Hell.

Can you understand these scriptures better now? If so, how then should we live?

Old Covenant believers are called righteous and warned to repent or suffer death. Again, this is not a physical death, but the Second Death. This confirms that the Old Covenant believers can lose the inheritance of the Kingdom, as we saw in Matthew 8:10-12.

Ezekiel 18:24-32

*But when a righteous man turns away from his righteousness and commits iniquity, and does according to all the abominations that the wicked man does, shall he live? All the righteousness which he has done shall not be remembered; because of the unfaithfulness of which he is guilty and the sin which he has committed, because of them **he shall die**. Yet you say, "The way of the LORD is not fair." Hear now, O house of Israel, is it not My way which is fair, and your ways which are not fair? When a righteous man turns away from his righteousness, com-mits iniquity**, and dies in it, it is because of the iniquity which he has done that he dies.** Again, when a wicked man turns away from the wickedness which he committed, and does what is lawful and right, he preserves himself alive. Because he considers and turns away from all the transgressions which he committed, **he shall surely live; he shall not die.** Yet the house of Israel says, "The way of the LORD is not fair." O house of Israel, is it not My ways which are fair, and your ways which are not fair?*

"Therefore I will judge you, O house of Israel, every one ac-cording to his ways," says the LORD God. "Repent, and turn from all your transgressions, so that iniquity will not be your ruin. Cast away from you all the transgressions which you have committed, and get yourselves a new heart and a new spirit. For why should you die, O house of Israel? For I have

no pleasure in the death of one who dies," says the LORD God. "Therefore turn and live!"

This scripture is repeated almost verbatim in Ezekiel 3:17-27 and Ezekiel 33:1-20, and the points are restated within each of the individual scriptures. The reason they were repeated is that the righteous were having a hard time receiving this word, which they believed was unfair. They believed it was not fair that the righteous should suffer the consequences of death for the unrepented sin in their life, and they didn't think it was fair that the unrighteous could live just by repenting.

In these verses, the Lord was trying to make the case to the righteous that His ways are not unfair and that they will be carried out just as He has repeatedly stated. The righteous find that it is appalling and mean spirited that the Lord would judge them worthy of the Second Death, but the Lord states that He takes no pleasure in the one who dies. These pharisaical righteous would rather pout about doctrine than just *turn and live*.

Hebrews 9:27

And as it is appointed for men to die once, but after this the judgment.

We know that everyone will die. That has been instituted by God and then judgment. It is not appointed for men to die twice. Whether a man (either a believer or nonbeliever) experiences the second death is dependant upon what that man chooses to do. For the believer, if one overcomes they will not be hurt by the second death (Revelation 2:11). This includes not living carnally (Romans 8:6), having faith with works (James 2:26), and fearing God (Matthew 10:28). For the unbeliever, if they do not believe in the saving work of Christ on the cross, they will perish (John 3:15-21).

CHAPTER 21

THIS SOUNDS LIKE PURGATORY

Many will say that the *"Gospel of the Kingdom"* sounds like the Catholic doctrine of Purgatory and will, therefore, disregard it out of hand, knowing the error of that teaching. It is because of this that we must take a closer look at the clear differences which separate the two.

We will see that the Catholic doctrine of Purgatory and the use of Indulgences to cancel one's suffering in Purgatory have distorted what Hell (*Gehenna*) actually is. We will see that the Catholic Church believes that there is an eternal punishment in the Lake of Fire and a temporal punishment which they call "Purgatory," which corresponds to what we have looked at as Hell (*Gehenna*) in our study. They get it right in that they distinguish between the two types of suffering, but their teaching goes downhill fast from there.

It will be clear when we study the doctrines of Purgatory and Indulgences of the Catholic Church just how aberrant these doctrines are in light of the Word of God. We will see that the Protestant Reformation was fueled by the disdain of a worldly church system which wielded its control and power through fear, manipulation and intimidation. The death of millions who stood up against this system should be evidence enough of the spirit in which it worked. I hope to show that the disdain the Reformers had for Purgatory and Indulgences led to the elimination of anything associated with the temporal punishment of purgatory. Hell and the Lake of Fire became synonymous, without distinction one from the other. The understanding of the two ages was condensed into one, with one judgment leading to either Heaven or the Lake of Fire. The importance of the "works" of men, including clergy and laity, were also eliminated for a faith-only understanding, which again severed ties to the corrupted church system the Protestants stood up against.

The word *purgatory* is not in the Bible. It is used by Catholics in reference to Hell (*Gehenna*). Hell is used by the Catholics (and many others) to describe the eternal wrath of God, which we have seen to be specifically the Lake of Fire. How these words are understood have a profound effect on whether people can understand the words of Jesus when He spoke of His Kingdom and Hell. In our concise study, we looked at three words for Hell in the New Testament and saw how they differed from each other and also how Hell differs from the Lake of Fire. We have become so acclimated to the use of Hell as being the Lake of Fire or eternal punishment that it is almost second nature to us. To highlight this fact, when quoting from other sources that use Hell to describe eternal punishment, I will add [the Lake of Fire] after Hell when it is used in this way:

> The Roman Catholic Church teaches that sin has a double conse-quence. For a member of the Catholic Church, committing a mortal (major) sin causes "eternal punishment," involving eternal separa-tion from God and suffering in Hell [the Lake of Fire]. The Catholic Church also teaches that under normal circumstances those who have not been baptized by either the Roman Catholic Church or an-other church teaching baptismal regeneration are also condemned to Hell [the Lake of Fire] because the stain of original sin remains upon their souls. Venial (minor) sin, in contrast, does not cause

"eternal punishment" but does cause "temporal punishment." Roman Catholic teachings sometimes refer to these "temporal punishments" given by God as a means of purifying His children (either in this life or in Purgatory). But the Roman Catholic Church also sees venial sins as creating a debt to God's justice that must be atoned for in a way that is distinct from Christ's atonement for eternal punishment. According to the Catechism of the Catholic Church, an indulgence is "the remission before God of the temporal punishment due to sin whose guilt has already been forgiven."[6]

Most Catholics are baptized as infants and believe that they receive salvation through the sacrament of Baptism, eliminating the stain of original sin. Catholics can lose their salvation if they have a mortal sin of which they have not repented and if they have not fulfilled the sacrament of Penance in accordance with Church guidelines. The sacrament of Penance is required **even** if one repents of a mortal sin, and it is this act that ensures members of their salvation, so as not to experience the eternal Lake of Fire.

It should be noted that there is a "temporal punishment" that must be paid for all venal (minor) sins that have been committed by a Catholic, **even** if they have been repented of. So, if you have a lustful thought, you will receive a specific punishment in Purgatory for that thought, whether you repent of it or not. If you have ten of those thoughts in one day, you will receive ten times the punishment, even if you repent. Every day one's sins are tabulated, not only those things that are done, but those things that should have been done. Can you feel the weight of that? As was noted above, the atoning work of Christ covers the eternal punishment of the believer but does not cover the punishment of venal sins that must be paid for in Purgatory. But wait, there is a solution!

A properly disposed member of the Christian faithful can obtain an Indulgence under prescribed conditions through the help of

6. https://www.gotquestions.org/plenary-indulgences.html

the Church, which, as the minister of redemption, dispenses and applies with authority the treasury of the satisfactions of Christ and the saints.[7]

In Roman Catholicism, the treasury of merit is the super-abundant store of righteousness and good works belonging to Christ, the Virgin Mary and the saints. The Treasury of Merit (it is also sometimes called the Treasury of Satisfaction, the Church's Treasury, or the *Thesaurus Ecclesiae*) is filled with the merit of Christ and Mary (who were sinless), and the saints, who had more than enough merit to enter Heaven themselves. They had earned more spiritual rewards than they needed. This merit is now available to others to "supplement" their own meritorious works.

According to the Catechism of the Catholic Church, "This treasury includes as well the prayers and good works of the Blessed Virgin Mary. They are truly immense, unfathomable, and even pristine in their value before God. In the treasury, too, are the prayers and good works of all the saints, all those who have followed in the footsteps of Christ the Lord and, by His grace, have made their lives holy and carried out the mission in the unity of the Mystical Body." [8]

And through apostolic succession from Peter, it is the Roman Catholic Church alone that has the authority to withdraw merit from this treasury and dispense it to believers in this life or in Purgatory, to atone for some or all of their venial sin. This it does through the granting of Catholic Indulgences.

Again, indulgences pertain only to temporal, not eternal, punishment and can only be distributed through a Roman Catholic

---

7. https://www.gotquestions.org/plenary-indulgences.html
8. https://www.gotquestions.org/treasury-of-merit.html

Church leader to someone who is either in Purgatory or is still living and whose soul is in the state of sanctifying grace (i.e., he/she would go to Purgatory, not Hell [the Lake of Fire], if he/she were to die at that moment). An indulgence can be obtained through a good deed done, a Mass being offered on behalf of someone, prayer, abstinence, giving to the poor, or some other meritorious act performed in accordance with requirements set by a Pope or bishop having jurisdiction over that individual. The offering of a Mass for someone is seen as one of the most effective means of reducing the temporal punishment of that person in Purgatory. An indulgence is partial if it removes part of the temporal punishment due to sin, or plenary if it removes all punishment."[9]

The history within the Catholic Church of issuing Indulgences is dreadful. An Indulgence was given after a cash payment was made to a clergyman, to eliminate or reduce one's time in Purgatory and, in fact, could be used for sins not yet committed. It was and is a get-out-of-purgatory card, and, like a debit card, you could use it for sinful living. The practice of taking cash for Indulgences was not eliminated officially by the Church until 1,567 AD. Until that time, it was used to fund the largest cathedrals and acquire countless art fortunes in the world. The Catholic Church acted more like the Mafia in that they took payments from those in their parishes for protection and threatened with eternal wrath those who refused to pay.

Today these cash payments have been replaced with charitable donations for special masses, saying the rosary, making contributions to the poor, doing works of service, etc. These acts can make one eligible to qualify for a reduction of suffering in Purgatory if authorized by a qualified agent of the Church. Without the aid of Indulgences, it is believed, one will suffer punishment for venial sins in Purgatory. One can receive a Plenary Indulgence, which will eliminate all punishment

9. https://www.gotquestions.org/plenary-indulgences.html

in Purgatory. You might want to keep the paperwork on that one. Indulgences can be used for you or others. I wish I was making this up.

There was and is no biblical basis to make such claims. They came from the mystical understanding of "enlightened clergy" who had convinced the lowly laity that they were endowed with the spiritual power to make such transactions. The Catholic belief in Apostolic Succession and the Infallibility of the Pope place the proclamations of the Church fathers and church traditions on the same footing as the Scriptures.

The belief in the Infallibility of the Pope came from the decree of a Pope. How insightful! Historically, Caesar, along with other Roman emperors, made similar proclamations about themselves.

Indulgences were more evident when I was growing up as a Roman Catholic, although they are making a comeback with encouragement from the most recent popes. I was trained by my grandmother to put coins into a metal box by the altar. We would light a candle and look adoringly at statues as we prayed. We prayed to Mary and the saints, who supposedly had omnipresent abilities to hear prayers and answer them or at least speak to those who could.

I would make confession to a priest in a confessional booth and be "absolved" of my sins through the sacrament of Penance. The priest would give me a specified number of Our Fathers and/or Hail Marys to be prayed that were commensurate with the amount of sins I had committed that week. Then I would leave the confessional booth and kneel at the altar to pray the prescribed prayers. These prayers were a required part of fulfilling the sacrament of Penance, so that I could be confident of being forgiven by God. Confession and repentance to the Lord directly wasn't enough.

Recently Pope Francis gave priests the ability to forgive the "mortal sins" of those who had repented for having abortions, an act once restricted to bishops and the Pope himself. This "grave sin" causes the excommunication of any Catholic, preventing them from receiving the sacraments of the Church and ultimately suffer eternal punishment [the Lake of Fire] unless the sacrament of Penance is performed by the appropriate agent of the Church. A woman repenting before God for the sin of abortion is not enough to prevent her from going to the Lake of Fire, despite the fact that she has put her faith in Christ. To prevent eternal torment, she must kneel before a priest and have that man lay hands on her while he speaks prayers to absolve her of her sins. This utter nonsense makes the blood of Christ of no effect without the approval of Church leaders who are ordained to wear fancy robes and ridiculously ornate hats.

The media has portrayed the Pope as one who is extending grace and mercy with such reforms, but the truth is that he is instilling fear and threatening those who have already repented with eternal damnation unless they follow the dictates of his Church. He has placed himself as an intermediary between God and man. He is declaring salvation and forgiveness over men, when that is the exclusive function of God alone. He will discover that fact when he ultimately stands before his Judge.

The laity, instead of confessing their sins to God and being washed from all iniquity, shame and guilt (which, by the way, is a free gift), are taught to perform these rituals and prayers on a continual basis in order to pay in full the debt of their sins.

1 John 1:9

*If we confess our sins, **He** is faithful and just to forgive us our sins and to cleanse us from all unrighteousness.*

The *"He"* in this verse does not refer to a member of the clergy. It refers to God alone.

1 Timothy 2:5

For there is one God and one Mediator between God and men, the Man Christ Jesus.

1 John 2:2

And He Himself is the propitiation for our sins, and not for ours only but also for the whole world.

It is the blood of Christ that atones for our sins, not the rituals adopted by men.

It is crucial to make a clear distinction between what Jesus meant when He warned His disciples about Hell (*Gehenna*) and what the Catholics believe Purgatory to be. The only similarity is that they are both a temporary place of punishment for carnal believers.

Unlike the Catholic doctrine, Jesus never stated that there would be punishment for sins that are already repented of. As I have shown earlier in Matthew 5, He warned the disciples that He would be judging the heart and not the outward appearance. He will judge lust in the heart as adultery and accusations and judgments as murder, and those found in that condition will go to Hell (*Gehenna*). These are standards that no man can measure up to without calling upon the mercy of the Lord. Jesus is not asking us to be without sin; He is calling us to humble ourselves and submit ourselves to His ways.

It was the religious leaders, who looked so righteous on the outside, who received the sharpest rebukes from Jesus.

Matthew 23:25-28

Woe to you, scribes and Pharisees, hypocrites! For you cleanse the outside of the cup and dish, but inside they are full of extortion and self-indulgence. Blind Pharisee, first cleanse the inside of the cup and dish, that the outside of them may be clean also.

Woe to you, scribes and Pharisees, hypocrites! For you are like white-washed tombs which indeed appear beautiful outwardly, but inside are full of dead men's bones and all uncleanness. Even so you also outwardly appear righteous to men, but inside you are full of hypocrisy and lawlessness.

Catholics believe that priests are reverent because they perform the sacraments of the Church, not unlike the scribes and Pharisees of old. Few practicing Catholics believe that priests will be judged as the Pharisees, and so it is not surprising that many Catholics look for the affirmation of priests in order to gain their security with God. They are more prone to be a "good Catholic" than to search their own hearts to be right with God. Many will be aghast to find that no representatives of the Church can advocate for them at the Judgment Seat. "But what about all my Indulgences?" These "doctrines of demons" have caused men to be blind to what the Word of God is saying to His people, and, as a consequence, not to be ready for His coming and have to suffer punishment.

Matthew 23:13

*But woe to you, scribes and Pharisees, hypocrites! For you **shut up the kingdom of heaven** against men; for you neither go in yourselves, nor do you allow those who are entering to go in.*

What is critical to see is that the understanding of the true meaning of Hell (*Gehenna*) was perverted and defiled by the leaders of the Catholic Church when they renamed it Purgatory and added man-made constructs to it. The doctrines of Purgatory brought them great wealth and control over all those under their authority. The carnality of the papacy and their doctrines would be clearly displayed when they justified and absolved the shedding of blood of any who opposed them.

The Protestant Reformation was a direct response to the policies of the Roman Catholic Church, in large part related to the doctrines of Purgatory and payments for Indulgences.

The Protestant Reformation was a widespread theological revolt in Europe against the abuses and totalitarian control of the Roman Catholic Church. Reformers such as Martin Luther in Germany, Ulrich Zwingli in Switzerland, and John Calvin in France protested various unbiblical practices of the Catholic Church and promoted a return to sound biblical doctrine. The precipitating event of the Protestant Reformation is generally considered to be Luther's posting of his Ninety-five Theses on the door of the Wittenberg Church on October 31, 1517.

The opposition to the false teaching of the Roman Catholic Church came to a head in the sixteenth century when Luther, a Roman Catholic monk, challenged the authority of the pope and, in particular, the selling of indulgences. Rather than heed the call to reform, the Roman Catholic Church dug in its heels and sought to silence the Reformers. [10]

When Martin Luther penned the Ninety-five Theses against corruption in the Catholic Church, he included over a dozen references about Purgatory, including: "They (the papacy) preach only human doctrines who say that as soon as the money clinks into the money chest, the soul flies out of purgatory."

Although Luther believed in Purgatory when he wrote the Theses, he was specifically attacking the church's doctrine regarding it. His position evolved until he refuted it in his later years when he was quoted as saying: "Hence the Pope has, also, invented purgatory and established his shameful annual market of masses. We may well see in this false doctrine and abomination

10. https://www.gotquestions.org/95-theses.html

as a fruit, that the foundation on which it is built, namely the Doctrine of the Migration of Souls, comes from the father of lies, the devil, who has deluded the people in the name of the dead.[11]

John Calvin stated: "Purgatory is a deadly fiction of Satan which nullifies the cross of Christ, inflicts unbearable contempt upon God's mercy, and overturns and destroys our faith." What does this Purgatory of theirs mean, other than the satisfaction that sin is paid for by the souls of the dead themselves. If it is perfectly clear that the blood of Christ is the sole satisfaction for sin, the sole expiation, the sole purgation, then what remains to say but that purgatory is a dreadful blasphemy against Christ.[12]

Eventually, new churches emerged from the Reformation, forming four major divisions of Protestantism: Luther's followers started the Lutheran Church, Calvin's followers started the Reformed Church, John Knox's followers started the Presbyterian Church in Scotland (using Calvinistic doctrine), and, later, Reformers in England started the Anglican Church.

The Reformers resisted the demands placed on them to recant these doctrines, even to the point of death. The five essential doctrines of the Protestant Reformation are as follows:

1. _Sola Scriptura_, "Scripture Alone." The Bible alone is the sole authority for all matters of faith and practice. Scripture and Scripture alone is the standard by which all teachings and traditions of the church must be measured. As Martin Luther so eloquently stated when told to recant his teachings, "Unless I am convinced by Scripture and plain reason — I do not accept

11. https://christianity.stackexchange.com/questions/43994/did-martin-luther-accept-or-reject-the-existence-of-purgatory/44049
12. https://theologyinverse.blogspot.com/2009/06/calvin-on-catholic-churches-teach-ing-of.html

the authority of the popes and councils, for they have contradicted each other—my conscience is captive to the Word of God. I cannot and I will not recant anything, for to go against conscience is neither right nor safe. God help me. Amen."

2. _Sola Gratia_, "Salvation by Grace Alone." Salvation is proof of God's undeserved favor; we are rescued from God's wrath by His grace alone, not by any work we do. God's blessing in Christ is the sole efficient cause of salvation. This grace is the supernatural work of the Holy Spirit who brings us to Christ by releasing us from our bondage to sin and raising us from spiritual death to spiritual life.

3. _Sola Fide_, "Salvation by Faith Alone." We are justified by faith in Christ alone, not by the works of the Law. It is by faith in Christ that His righteousness is imputed to us as the only possible satisfaction of God's perfect standard.

4. _Solus Christus_, "In Christ Alone." Salvation is found in Jesus Christ alone; no one and nothing else can save. Jesus' substitutionary death on the cross is sufficient for our justification and reconciliation to God the Father. The Gospel has not been preached if Christ's redemption is not declared and if faith in His resurrection is not solicited.

5 - _Soli Deo Gloria_, "For the Glory of God Alone." Salvation is of God and has been accomplished by God for His glory alone. As Christians, we must magnify Him always and live our lives in His presence, under His authority and for His glory.[13]

These doctrines were in response to the abuses of the Catholic Church. The way they are written states not only what the Reformers believed, but also what they renounced. Scripture was to be the sole authority for matters regarding faith and practice. This was a repudia-

13. https://www.gotquestions.org/Protestant-Reformation.html

tion of the Catholic belief that the sayings of the Pope were equal to the Scriptures. The doctrine that salvation was through faith alone and not by any work we do was in response to the Catholic Church doctrines and rituals that would require parishioners to do works in order to earn their salvation. Salvation by Christ alone was a way to renounce the Catholic understanding that forgiveness of sins could come from payments for Indulgences and the sacrament of Penance. Declaring that salvation is of God and for His glory only was opposing the glorification of the papacy through all its regal pageantry and decrees of infallibility.

These five doctrines were so polarizing that they were like "acts of war." They would cause the death of those who believed in them and would inspire those who believed in them to go to war. It is painful to think that millions were killed over doctrines to determine what it meant to be Christ-like.

During the Protestant Reformation, certain Protestant theologians developed a view of salvation (soteriology) that excluded Purgatory. This was in part a result from a doctrinal change concerning justification and sanctification on the part of the Reformers. In Catholic theology, one is made righteous by a progressive infusion of divine grace accepted through faith and cooperated with through good works; however, in Martin Luther's doctrine, justification rather meant "the declaring of one to be righteous," where God imputes the merits of Christ upon one who remains without inherent merit. In this process, good works done in faith (i.e. through Penance) are more of an unessential by-product that contribute nothing to one's own state of righteousness; hence, in Protestant theology, "becoming perfect" came to be understood as an instantaneous act of God and *not* a process or journey of purification that continues in the afterlife. Thus, Protestant soteriology developed the view that each one of the elect (saved) experienced instantaneous glorification upon death. As such, there was little reason to pray for the dead. [14]

What we see quite frequently is that when there is a reaction against an extreme, the response tends to move to the other extreme. The Reformers were so repulsed by the many works that were instituted by the Catholic Church that they negated the fact that any works at all were required of a believer. Calvin would go so far as to say that a believer would not be capable of choosing or believing in God because of the "total depravity of man." Calvinists would further believe that salvation would come because God had "elected" one to believe, and that this would not come from any virtue, good works or faith of those elected, but it would be at God's sole discretion. Jesus, they believed, died for the elect only. He did not die for the sins of the entire world. Jesus only bore the sins of the elect. Therefore, there is a "limited atonement."

It's not that the blood of Jesus would not have the ability to save, but that God decreed to love some and hate others and, thus, limit the atonement of His blood. An "irresistible grace" would be upon the lives of the elect to transform them into saving faith. Nothing could stop the sovereign will of God. The "perseverance of the saints" is guaranteed. There is nothing that **one can do or not do** that would prevent the elect from receiving any suffering for their actions. Although Calvinists believe that they should evangelize out of obedience to the Scriptures, they know that no "work" of men can influence the election that has already been ordained by God. Repentance and good works are encouraged and anticipated, but, ultimately, they cannot supersede the state of righteousness that has been decreed by God on the elect.

We see that the Reformers eliminated the need for believers to do

14. https://en.wikipedia.org/wiki/Reformation

any works through their new doctrine. Salvation would come from "faith alone," and that faith was given by God to those who were predestined to believe. When believers died, they would go directly to Heaven, since they would be in their perfect state. There would be no sin in a believer's life to judge, since God had sovereignly atoned for their every sin. The only thing to be determined at the Judgment Seat of Christ would be how many rewards the believer received. Although rewards or the lack thereof are based on what one does or does not do, this was not considered "works righteousness."

The Reformers eliminated all sin in a believer's life, whether they lived a carnal life or not, and, thus, eliminated the need for repentance and any punishment for unconfessed sin. The only ones who would suffer punishment were the unbelievers, those not elected and, with that, Purgatory was eliminated and Hell (*Gehenna*) came to mean the Lake of Fire. Do you see how Hell (*Gehenna*) was lost?

Let me state this again: The only ones who would suffer punishment were the unbelievers or those not elected and, with that, Purgatory was eliminated and Hell (*Gehenna*) came to mean the Lake of Fire.

It is easy to be repulsed by what Purgatory has become within the Roman Catholic Church, but I would suggest that the true understanding of Hell (*Gehenna*) was also lost by the Reformers. The proverbial baby was thrown out with the bath water. The Protestant reaction to the excesses of the Roman Catholic Church led to its own imbalance. The Roman Catholic priests absolving the laity through their rituals was replaced with some Protestant bishops absolving their congregants of any punishment through their doctrine.

In Matthew 5, Jesus was bringing forth a New Covenant in which He declared that He would be judging the hearts of the righteous and not their outward appearance. He said that those who had murdered and lusted in their heart would be sent to Hell (*Gehenna*). Does it make sense that He was talking about the Lake of Fire? The Reformers believed in the eternal security of the believer, which could not be lost, yet these New Covenant guidelines indicated the opposite, if Hell (*Gehenna*) was translated into the Lake of Fire. Jesus was calling His people to repent in their hearts or else there would be a punishment that they would experience. God's people are not without sin. That is why He calls us to repent. The Pharisees thought they were above reproach, and they killed the prophets who said they were not.

Why should believers fear the Lord if there is no punishment? Does one fear the Lord because of the possibility of losing rewards? Does that make anyone tremble? Why would Jesus say,"If you don't forgive, then you won't be forgiven?" Why would He call most of the seven churches in Revelation 2 and 3 to repentance and delineate the consequences for their not obeying? Why would He exhort the righteous to be ready?

The belief that Hell (*Gehenna*) is the same as the Lake of Fire has produced a problem on the opposite side of the doctrinal spectrum. Believers from the Armenian viewpoint believe that anyone can exercise their free will and come to faith in Jesus. They understand the stern biblical warnings of punishment toward the believer who rebels and backslides. Unfortunately, they see the fiery punishment to be the Lake of Fire instead of Hell (*Gehenna*). They believe that the inheritance of eternal life (New Heaven and New Earth) that comes by faith can be lost and, thus, a Christian can suffer eternal wrath in the Lake of Fire.

It's not hard to feel the weight of being separated from God forever because one judges someone or lusts in one's heart. Would a father punish His son forever because he stole something in the 5th grade? God is a righteous judge and faithful to His promises, even if we are not. The promise of eternal life is given despite how backslidden we become. Salvation comes by faith and not by works, lest any man boast. Understanding the difference between Hell (*Gehenna*) and the Lake of Fire can be quite liberating.

On the other hand, there are many who disregard both Hell (*Gehenna*) and the Lake of Fire—at their peril. I would suggest that the present hyper-grace movement has an imbalance that places an overwhelming emphasis on the grace and saving power of God without the clear delineation of the consequences of sin and the need for ongoing repentance. I want to emphasize that I do not want to diminish the grace and mercy of God by any means. God, in His love for us, has called us to be His Bride, and yet He calls His Bride to *"make herself ready."* The prophetic warnings of God to His wayward people have always been rooted in love, so that His people would avert coming judgment and live with Him.

Romans 11:22

Therefore consider the goodness and severity of God: on those who fell, severity; but toward you, goodness, if you continue in His goodness. Otherwise you also will be cut off.

The vast majority of the Christian denominations distinguish themselves by either believing that salvation comes from "faith alone" or by a "works" emphasis. I would suggest that when folks understand the different inheritances for believers, it becomes clear how the Scriptures regarding faith and works harmonize with one another and do not contradict.

Doctrines that believe in one judgment for believers are left with only the choice of Heaven or the Lake of Fire, since the meaning of Hell (*Gehenna*) has been lost.

Mark 7:13

making the word of God of no effect through your tradition which you have handed down. And many such things you do.

These systems of thought have caused blindness upon believers that prevents them from understanding the parables and understanding what Jesus meant when He warned His disciples of Hell (*Gehenna*) fire. I desire only God's best for my brothers and sisters in Christ.

Chapter 22

The Letter to the Laodicean Church

Revelation 3:14-22

And to the angel of the church of the Laodiceans write,

"These things says the Amen, the Faithful and True Witness, the Beginning of the creation of God: 'I know your works, that you are neither cold nor hot. I could wish you were cold or hot. So then, because you are lukewarm, and neither cold nor hot, I will vomit you out of My mouth. Because you say, "I am rich, have become wealthy, and have need of nothing"—and do not know that you are wretched, miserable, poor, blind, and naked—I counsel you to buy from Me gold refined in the fire, that you may be rich; and white garments, that you may be clothed, that the shame of your nakedness may not be revealed; and anoint your eyes with eye salve, that you may see. As many as I love, I rebuke and chasten. Therefore be zealous and repent. Behold, I stand at the door and knock. If anyone hears My voice and opens the door, I will come in to him and dine with him, and he with Me. To him who overcomes I will grant to sit with Me on My throne, as I also overcame and sat down with My Father on His throne.'"

He who has an ear, let him hear what the Spirit says to the churches.

The Laodicean Church was neither hot nor cold, but was luke-warm. These people had once been hot but they had cooled down. This condition was similar to what the church in Ephesus experienced.

Revelation 2:4-5

Nevertheless I have this against you, that you have left your first love. Remember therefore from where you have fallen; repent and do the first works,

It would be better if they had been cold because at least it would be evident what bad shape they were in. Because they were luke-warm (and still going to church), they were clueless to their actual condition.

Revelation 3:16

So then, because you are lukewarm, and neither cold nor hot, I will vomit you out of My mouth.

Jesus will vomit the church out of his mouth. A tamer version says, "Spit," but this is a profound statement. We don't spit in our houses; we spit outside, and if we vomit, we flush it down the drain. A question that seems obvious to ask is this: "Where will you **land if you are spit out?**" If the people were judged in their present condition, they would be spit out of God's mouth, so they should repent. This is another depart-from-Me moment, and now, from our study, we know where they will land. This stern warning, as spoken, should quicken the American church today, but will modern believers hear it?

These first-century people said they were *"rich."* This could mean that they had plenty of possessions, warehouses full, sort of like us today. And the tragedy is that all of our wealth has no heavenly value. As a matter of fact, it reveals covetous hearts and a lack of love for the needy. In fact, those who thought themselves to be rich were actually wretched, miserable and poor.

1 John 3:17

But whoever has this world's goods, and sees his brother in need, and shuts up his heart from him, how does the love of God abide in him?

Jesus said that we should ask for gold refined by fire. Fire purifies gold. That's the only way you can get the impurities out of it. So you skim off the dross and cast it aside.

Fire means suffering trials and tribulations that are (take note) good for us. What is in us is revealed when we go through difficulties. Does the church of today embrace the fire required for holiness? Or does it continually burn and strive for the riches of this world?

Then Jesus said:

Buy from me ... white garments, that you may be clothed, that the shame of your nakedness may not be revealed; and anoint your eyes with eye salve, that you may see.

The people of the church of Laodicea thought they were dressed sharply and thought they could see clearly, but Jesus told them to buy eye salve so that they might see. Have you tried telling someone who thinks they see that they don't really see? It's not hard to imagine a response like, "I see just fine; it's the church down the street that can't see."

We have many Bibles (some of us have every translation), we have commentaries which help us understand both the Greek and Hebrew texts, and we've heard so many sermons, listened to so much Christian radio and TV that we have the answer before the question is finished. We have *heard that* and done that before. We know it all, have argued the arguments, gotten certifications and degrees, and yet we are still blind. If you think you see everything, then why would you need eye salve? What is it you don't see? Get some eye salve and find out.

It was not that their garments were dirty; it was that they were naked and didn't know it. They needed white garments to cover their nakedness/sin. What does that mean? It means they thought their sins were covered by the blood, that it was "all under the blood," but it was not. Let this verse reshape your theology. This is why we need to repent and be ready for the coming of Jesus.

Let me give an Old Testament example of this:

Exodus 12:21-23

Then Moses called for all the elders of Israel and said to them, "Pick out and take lambs for yourselves according to your families, and kill the Passover lamb. And you shall take a bunch of hyssop, dip it in the blood that is in the basin, and strike the lintel and the two doorposts with the blood that is in the basin. And none of you shall go out of the door of his house until morning. For the LORD will pass through to strike the Egyptians; and when He sees the blood on the lintel and on the two doorposts, the LORD will pass over the door and not allow the destroyer to come into your houses to strike you."

It would have been foolhardy for an Israelite to not physically apply the blood to the lintel and the two doorposts as instructed by Moses. The instructions were very clear, specific and doable, but they required obedience. In this case, disobedience by God's people would have had fatal consequences.

The blood of Christ was shed for the sins of the world, but it will only affect those who apprehend it. Some believers think that every sin they commit is "under the blood," and because of it, there is no need to repent. Some are so confident in this that for them to repent would be an act of unbelief. They believe they are already forgiven. Make no mistake: any sin, no matter how vile or hidden, **can and will** be forgiven without limit, but only for those who repent. Knowing you should repent is different from actually repenting, and both have starkly different ramifications.

1 John 1:9

If we confess our sins, He is faithful and just to forgive us our sins and to cleanse us from all unrighteousness.

"*If*" is the key word here. God will not force anyone to repent. The writings to the church at Laodicea continues:

Revelation 3:19

As many as I love, I rebuke and chasten. Therefore be zealous and repent.

Jesus brought to light the true condition of the church. He rebukes and chastens those whom He loves. Make no mistake: consequences will come upon all who fail to repent. Christ is a righteous judge and will be exacting in His sentencing. Pursue repentance now! It's up to you. Don't be slack in this matter. Be zealous.

And then the most incredible thing happened. Jesus showed us what repentance is:

Revelation 3:20

Behold, I stand at the door and knock. If anyone hears My voice and opens the door, I will come in to him and dine with him, and he with Me.

It is the kindness of God that draws us to repentance, and we can see this through this verse. Jesus is gently pursuing us, by knocking on the door and calling to us. This door is like the entry into the chambers of our heart. The closed door is like sin which separates us from the Lord. Jesus doesn't bang the door down or walk through a wall, although He could, but He waits for us to open the door. He is persistent, yet whether He comes in or not is entirely dependent upon us.

Unfortunately, many keep the door closed. Some are afraid to open the door because they are ashamed of the mess inside. When the Lord knocks at their door, they ask, "Could you come back next week? The house is a mess." Unfortunately, our efforts to clean up fail miserably without the Lord, and shame causes us to keep asking for extensions. How about tomorrow? This goes on ... until many ignore the knock by turning up the Christian music, keeping busy doing good works, getting lost in addictions or just giving up. Some would rather be in charge of their own kingdom and are doing quite well (thank you very much). Some bolt the door shut, fearing that God is like their earthly father, who will abuse them or who has an uncontrollable temper, so He is kept outside.

What is it in us that keeps our doors shut? Jesus called out:

Matthew 23:37

O Jerusalem, Jerusalem, the one who kills the prophets and stones those who are sent to her! How often I wanted to gather your children together, as a hen gathers her chicks under her wings, but you were not willing!

Our Lord is not mean and vindictive; He is long-suffering, patient, merciful and compassionate. The warnings of impending judgment can make one afraid and cause them to close the door, but a true fear of the Lord causes one to humble themselves, trust in God, open the door by faith and be restored. When we are afraid, we trust ourselves to protect ourselves. When we have a fear of the Lord, we trust in God and His mercies to restore us. He desires to bring light and healing to places of darkness and wounding, but we must trust in Him for this to happen. Don't be afraid, Open the door.

Jesus said, *"I will come in to him and dine with him, and he with Me."* Pinch yourself right now because Jesus desires to be with you. Notice how this verse reads, *"I will come in to him and dine with him, and he with Me."* The Lord is just not coming in to be served, like at a restaurant *(dine with him)*, but He desires for us to be at the table with Him *(and he with Me)*. When we repent, we then have fellowship with God.

Let's continue:

Revelation 3:21-22

To him who overcomes I will grant to sit with Me on My throne, as I also overcame and sat down with My Father on His throne.
He who has an ear, let him hear what the Spirit says to the churches.

Jesus wants us to sit with Him on His throne. This is our inheritance. Among the church, there are those who will receive and others who will not receive this gift, based upon whether or not they are overcomers. God doesn't expect us to be without sin, but as we repent and walk by faith, we *are* overcomers.

Revelation 12:11, KJV

And they overcame him by the blood of the Lamb, and by the word of their testimony; and they loved not their lives unto the death.
"He who has an ear, let him hear what the Spirit says to the churches."

181

Now, at first glance, when looking at how Jesus spoke to the Laodicean Church, it might seem as though there were two Jesuses talking. One of them was stern ("I'm about to vomit you out of My mouth"), and the other was kinder and gentler ("Sit with me on My throne"). But this is who God is. He is a God of justice, and He is a God of mercy. These two very different attributes in Him are not in conflict with one another.

God is not eighty percent justice and twenty percent mercy or thirty percent justice and seventy percent mercy. He is one hundred percent of both. He is the fullness of justice and the fullness of mercy. We tend to view Him one way or the other because it is difficult for us to reconcile these seemingly-opposing aspects. The revelation of the goodness and mercies of God must not be watered down. We must know it in its fullness. But, in the same way, we need to know the fear of the Lord. Mercy and justice can be like inhaling and exhaling. Both are required for living. We would never argue that one of them was better than the other.

Romans 11:20-22

Well said. Because of unbelief they were broken off, and you stand by faith. Do not be haughty, but fear. For if God did not spare the natural branches, He may not spare you either. Therefore **consider the goodness and severity of God**: *on those who fell, severity; but toward you, goodness,* **if** *you continue in His goodness. Otherwise you also will be cut off.*

Now, before we go further, I want to refocus us, so that we don't concentrate on what we *are not* but on who we *are* in Christ. I remember a time of frustration in my walk when I seemed to do nothing right. When I read the following verse, my heart would sink:

John 14:15, ESV

If you love me, you will keep my commandments.

This saddened my heart because I clearly was not obeying, and this seemed to mean that I clearly did not love Him. I could almost feel the weight of guilt on my heart. Then I was impressed with a thought that wasn't mine. "You're reading it the wrong way." **IF** *you love me, you* **WILL** *keep my commandments.* Suddenly, there was a paradigm shift. If I concentrated on loving God, then I would obey Him instead of trying to do good to prove that I loved Him. I concentrated on opening the door so that I could be loved and so that I could love Him back. And, as I was loved, I could love my neighbor as myself. Let's focus on *being* not on *doing*.

CHAPTER 23

DIVORCE AND REMARRIAGE

I want to take some time to talk about divorce and remarriage and give some insights that we can gather from our study into the Gospel of the Kingdom. I know that this is a sensitive topic because it can stir up hurts, anger and shame that often run deep and wide. My intent is to bring healing to those areas and not to point a finger or condemn. We must let the Scriptures guide us.

There are many differing viewpoints on divorce and remarriage, ranging from one being able to remarry indefinitely for any reason at all without consequence, to believing that one will end up in the Lake of Fire if they divorce and remarry. I would venture to say that many Christians are unclear as to the exact consequences of these actions and just hope for the best for themselves and others.

Please allow me to give a relatively brief overview of this topic, knowing this will just scratch the surface and require us to look more fully at the Scriptures at a later time.

First, let's see what the Word of God says on this subject:

Romans 7:1-3

Or do you not know, brethren (for I speak to those who know the law), that the law has dominion over a man as long as he lives? For the woman who has a husband is bound by the law to her husband as long as he lives. But if the husband dies, she is released from the law of her husband. So then if, while her husband lives, she marries another man, she will be called an adulteress; but if her husband dies, she is free from that law, so that she is no adulteress, though she has married another man.

These words form the basis for the marriage vows that we say today:

I_____ take_____ to be my wife, to have and to hold from this day forward; for better, for worse; for richer, for poorer; in sickness and in health; to love, to honor and to cherish for all the days of our lives, until death do us part.

This last phrase, "until death do us part," is a part of every marriage vow made, yet there are obviously many who divorce before their spouse dies. There are many reasons people use to justify getting a divorce, but they all require one to break the vow: "until death do us part."

Unfortunately, the State has instituted what is called "no-fault divorce," which allows one to divorce and remarry for any reason and as many times as one desires. This nullifies the until-death-do-us-part clause and renders it meaningless. The Supreme Court also has now allowed for the marriage of homosexuals. This further distorts God's intention that marriage be between a man and a woman in a life-long covenant. Most of us are so deeply influenced by the cultural norms regarding divorce and remarriage that God's Word can seem stark and archaic to us. However, if we follow His ways, it will produce healthy, loving families.

Paul wrote to the Corinthian believers:

1 Corinthians 7:11

But even if she does depart, let her remain unmarried or be reconciled to her husband. And a husband is not to divorce his wife.

185

We see here that if there is a separation, a spouse is either to remain unmarried or to reconcile with her husband. This further reinforces the vow of "until death do us part."

Jesus taught the same thing:

Mark 10:11-12

So He said to them, "Whoever divorces his wife and marries another commits adultery against her. And if a woman divorces her husband and marries another, she commits adultery."

And what is the consequence of a believer being found in adultery? You might be hard pressed to get an answer to that question from most modern-day clergy. So, should these warnings of Jesus be ignored or shrugged off just because our modern culture has chosen a different path?

Jesus further stated:

Matthew 5:27-32

"You have heard that it was said to those of old, 'You shall not commit adultery.' But I say to you that whoever looks at a woman to lust for her has already committed adultery with her in his heart. If your right eye causes you to sin, pluck it out and cast it from you; for it is more profitable for you that one of your members perish, than for your whole body to be cast into hell. And if your right hand causes you to sin, cut it off and cast it from you; for it is more profitable for you that one of your members perish, than for your whole body to be cast into hell.

Furthermore it has been said, 'Whoever divorces his wife, let him give her a certificate of divorce.' But I say to you that whoever divorces his wife for any reason except sexual immorality causes her to commit adultery; and whoever marries a woman who is divorced commits adultery."

We can only unlock what Jesus is saying if we know about the "Gospel of the Kingdom." As we have seen, these are the New Covenant standards that Jesus will be using to judge believers at the Judgment Seat of Christ.

If one lusts in their heart, they could be subject to Hell fire. If one holds unforgiveness or judges another, they could be subject to Hell fire. If one is a worship leader and sleeps with his girl friend, he could be subject to Hell fire. If one watches Internet pornography, they could be subject to Hell fire. If one has an abortion or condones the taking of innocent life, they could be subject to Hell fire. If one divorces and remarries while their spouse is still living, they could be subject to Hell fire.

Jesus was very forthright in revealing what He considered to be sin and what the consequences would be for those who disobeyed. Was His purpose to condemn? Never. His purpose was to warn those who are in sin so that they could repent and not suffer for it.

In a very real sense, it is impossible for us to meet the standards Jesus has set forth without falling short. He knew this but has made every provision by His blood that we might be cleansed from all iniquity. For those who ignore His words or justify their actions, there will be righteous judgment.

"But what about that 'exception clause?'" many ask. Here it is again:

> But I say to you that whoever divorces his wife **for any reason except** sexual immorality (porneia) causes her to commit adultery; and whoever marries a woman who is divorced commits adultery.

There is only **one** reason that allows a person to remarry without it being considered adultery, and that is described by the Greek word *porneia*. This word is translated in some versions as *fornication* or *sexual immorality*. This is interesting in that fornication means sexual relations

187

between persons who are not married. It would seem that the word *porneia* should be translated as *adultery*, which is illicit sexual activity by a married person, but not one of the many English translations uses the word *adultery* here. What illicit sexual activity could a couple engage in that would not be adultery? What is *porneia* referring to?

There are two translations, the American Standard Version and the Revised Standard Version, that give us a clue.

Matthew 5:32, RSV

> *But I say to you that every one who divorces his wife, except on the ground of **unchastity**, makes her an adulteress; and whoever marries a divorced woman commits adultery.*

What is *unchastity*? *Unchastity* is "having sexual relations before marriage," which would make a bride unchaste or no longer a virgin. Part of the Jewish wedding ceremony was for the man to have sexual relations with his bride to confirm that she was indeed a virgin. The first act of sexual intercourse for a woman would cause the hymen to break, and there would be an issuance of blood. This is not a fail-safe test, but it was the one used at the time.

There are passages in Deuteronomy 22 which speak of the cloth with blood stains, which was used as proof of a bride's virginity. If the bride was found not to be a virgin, the groom could actually choose to annul the marriage.

It is easy for our culture to miss what Jesus was saying about virginity within the context of a traditional Jewish wedding ceremony. The only vestige of the importance of chastity in marriage today is the white wedding dress. For centuries, it has represented purity or virginity.

We see an example of this concept in the story of Joseph and Mary. It seemed to Joseph that Mary had committed *porneia*, having sexual relations before marriage, since she was pregnant. If that were true, then Joseph was free to divorce her and marry another, and he would not have committed adultery. Although Joseph and Mary were technically not married yet, there would be a need for divorce because the Jewish betrothal agreement was legally binding.

What Jesus was saying is hidden unless you know the context of the Jewish wedding. Within our culture, a divorce is only needed after the actual wedding ceremony is performed. The engagement proposal with the giving of the ring is not legally binding. Jesus stated His intention for marriage and said that divorce and remarriage was adultery except for the case of unchastity (*porneia*).

Didn't God divorce Israel?

The Lord betrothed Himself to Israel:

Hosea 2:19-20

> *I will betroth you to Me forever;*
> *Yes, I will betroth you to Me*
> *In righteousness and justice,*
> *In lovingkindness and mercy;*
> *I will betroth you to Me in faithfulness,*
> *And you shall know the LORD.*

The Lord also divorced Israel because of her ongoing adulteries after repeated warnings from the prophets:

Jeremiah 3:8

> *Then I saw that for all the causes for which backsliding Israel had committed adultery, I had put her away and given her **a certificate of divorce**; yet her treacherous sister Judah did not fear, but went and played the harlot also.*

Israel had been split into two kingdoms—Israel and Judah. Although both kingdoms were backslidden and playing the harlot, it was to Israel that God gave a certificate of divorce. We should note that this divorce happened during the betrothal period, since the wedding would not have happened until the end of this age. A divorce was needed to break the betrothal agreement between God and Israel. This confirms that God's standard is that there can be a divorce only for the reason of unchastity.

When Jesus died on the cross, He was free from the betrothal contract with Israel and was, thus, legally capable of becoming betrothed to Israel again (which He will do, thus fulfilling all the promises He has made to them). God's amazing plan of redemption for Israel reveals His faithfulness, despite Israel's faithlessness.

Now, I want to look at the exchange Jesus had with the Pharisees and His disciples in Matthew 19:

Matthew 19:9-10, RSV

"And I say to you: whoever divorces his wife, except for unchastity (porneia), and marries another, commits adultery."
The disciples said to him, "If such is the case of a man with his wife, it is not expedient to marry."

As we can see here, Jesus clearly showed His disciples that the only exception in marriage was unchastity (*porneia*). This caused those disciples to say that it was better never to marry. They understood exactly what Jesus was saying. His words included the thought that even if your wife committed adultery, you still could not lawfully divorce her and marry another. This was an appalling idea to the disciples.

Matthew 19:11-12, RSV

But he said to them, "Not all men can receive this saying, but only those to whom it is given. For there are eunuchs who have been so from birth, and there are eunuchs who have been made eunuchs by men, and there are eunuchs who have made themselves eunuchs for the sake of the kingdom of heaven. He who is able to receive this, let him receive it."

Jesus responded to the disciples, telling them of three different types of eunuch. What is a eunuch? A eunuch is a man who has been castrated and cannot, therefore, reproduce. Jesus said that there are eunuchs who are born that way (meaning that some have a congenital defect that makes them eunuchs).

There is another type of eunuch, one that is made that way by man. In Israel, some servants were purposely made eunuchs and then set to watch over the king's harem. It was thought that they would be more submissive to their rulers as eunuchs.

Then there are some who make themselves eunuchs for the sake of the Kingdom of Heaven. Jesus was saying that it would be better to make yourself a eunuch than to divorce and remarry. If one divorced and remarried, they would be found in adultery at the Judgment Seat of Christ and, therefore, would miss the Kingdom of Heaven.

This is analogous to Matthew 5:29, where Jesus warned the disciples that it would be better for them to pluck out their eye (which speaks of lusting) or to cut off their hand (which represents pointing in judgment at someone or actually striking them) than to be found in sin and end up in Hell. Jesus was using these vivid examples, not to promote self-mutilation, but to drive home the severity of the judgment that will come for those who disobey.

In our study on the Kingdom, we have seen that a believer will be judged as to whether they go into the Kingdom of Heaven or to Hell (*Gehenna*), and we see that these two scriptures confirm what we propose will happen at the Judgment Seat. Jesus was clearly showing His New Covenant standard for marriage.

Now, the big question to those who have divorced and remarried would be: what should you do now? First of all, Jesus spoke very directly about our sin, not to condemn us, but to cause us to turn to Him.

It is His mercy to warn us of His righteous judgment that is coming. So, don't try to justify what you've done. Acknowledge that your ways are not His ways, that you have done what you thought was right in your own sight. Confess your sin of adultery to the living God, and be confident that He will forgive you.

Knowing you should ask for forgiveness and actually doing it are two different things, and the two have starkly different consequences. Confess with your mouth and believe in your heart. Take time to do this.

Remember, what you did was legal to do, but it was contrary to God's view on marriage. I have personally disregarded God's standards and have married people who were divorced. I know now that I gave them bad counsel, and I have repented for doing that. But, no matter what we do, Jesus will forgive us—if we confess our sins to Him.

After you repent, listen to what else God would have you to do.

Jesus protected a woman caught in adultery and spoke to her accusers. *"He who is without sin,"* He said, *"throw the first stone"*:

John 8:10-11

When Jesus had raised Himself up and saw no one but the woman, He said to her, "Woman, where are those accusers of yours? Has no one condemned you?"
She said, "No one, Lord."
And Jesus said to her, "Neither do I condemn you; go and sin no more."

This is the New Covenant standard for dealing with the sin of adultery.

Paul wrote to the Corinthian Church to give counsel to new believers who were in a variety of situations. There were new believers who were married to unbelievers, and they were asking what they should do. There were slaves asking if they could now go free. There were those who were separated from their spouses asking if they could remarry. Paul gave them some sage advice:

1 Corinthians 7:24 and 26-27

Brethren, let each one remain with God in that state in which he was called. ...
I suppose therefore that this is good because of the present distress—that it
is good for a man to remain as he is: Are you bound to a wife? Do not seek
to be loosed. Are you loosed from a wife? Do not seek a wife.

There will be many who are divorced and remarried who will understand for the first time what God's true intention for marriage is. I believe that those who are divorced and remarried should be bound to the wife they have now and not seek to be loosed. Those who are divorced and who have a living spouse should not seek another wife.

As we noted above, Jesus told the adulterous woman to *"sin no more,"* and I believe that means to stay with the one you are with "until death do [you] part." It seems that this is how God would respond to those who repent. It seems also a way to keep families together, families who have already felt the brokenness that comes with divorce. There are hosts of varying circumstances that individuals have been through which will require that each one seek the Lord and be convinced in their own heart as to what they should do. Ultimately, each one will stand before God alone and be judged.

As we discussed earlier, there is a lot of pain that comes with divorce. This pain is experienced, not only by the spouses, but also by the children and the extended family. The task is to bring healing to every aspect of the divorce.

We saw, in the Parable of the Unforgiving Servant, how much Jesus was angered by unforgiveness. He hates divorce because of the devastation it causes to the family of God. He will break the curse of adultery off of those who repent. He wants to set them free from every accusation, bitterness, hopelessness, anger and depression. Those who repent of adultery before God will then be empowered to repent to all they have offended and for all the gossip and slander their actions have brought on. There is no justification for holding resentment and/or harboring bitterness. The Lord will take off all shame and guilt. Love will flourish in relationships which have been devoid of it.

Children will need to be discipled so that they take no sides and are not allowed to dishonor their parents for the bad choices they have made. Instead, they should be taught to pray for each parent earnestly (despite their shortcomings) and expect to see the glory of the Lord bring restoration and deliverance.

The Lord calls us to pray for our enemies and bless those who curse us. This is not a suggestion; it is a command. He has also given us the ministry of reconciliation. This will provide a great opportunity to share the Gospel and see hearts healed. It is imperative that your heart be pure toward your ex spouse.

1 Corinthians 7:16

For how do you know, O wife, whether you will save your husband? Or how do you know, O husband, whether you will save your wife?

God can make a stony heart into a heart of flesh. Remember, we will all be judged in the same way we judge others.

The coming revival will bring restoration to broken families so that the following scriptural promise will be fulfilled:

Malachi 4:6

And he will turn
The hearts of the fathers to the children,
And the hearts of the children to their fathers,
Lest I come and strike the earth with a curse.

I know this is a concise outline and would suggest some expanded writings available at www.thekingdomofheavenislike.com.

Chapter 24

Being Ready for Tribulation

I have proposed to you that the Body of Christ will suffer great persecution in the last days and that the saints will be resurrected before the Bowl Judgments, which will be the wrath of God on the unbelievers who are left on the Earth. Many, including myself, may be surprised how things actually unfold, but it is incumbent upon us to be ready for Christ's coming.

I want to take issue with the popular belief that there will be a pretribulation rapture and that believers will be taken up and away before the tribulation. I'm not interested in taking a lot of time to argue one way or another, but I think that believers are being lulled into a false sense of security if they understand that, once things start getting violent, they will be taken away from it all. Is the American church ready to suffer, endure and persevere even before the tribulation? The hardest form of suffering some saints endure is to wait in a long line at the Sunday buffet.

Isn't it either naïve or foolish to tell saints in hostile countries that we will miss the tribulation, when they are being beheaded, imprisoned and having their churches burned down now? There are estimates that one hundred thousand believers are killed for their faith every year. How many of them are from the U.S.?

When American missionaries are in danger overseas, the vast majority of times they are pulled out of harm's way, and the nationals stay, continue the work and pay the price. Could it be that the American pre-trib-rapture doctrine allows us to live our Christian lives very safely and comfortably without feeling guilty? Is it just part of our Prosperity Gospel?

Let's see what will happen to the saints during the time when the Beast will arrive on the scene at the end of this age:

Revelation 13:7

It was granted to him [the Beast] *to **make war with the saints** and to overcome them. And authority was given him over every tribe, tongue, and nation.*

Revelation 13:5-10, ESV

And the beast was given a mouth uttering haughty and blasphemous words, and it was allowed to exercise authority for forty-two months. It opened its mouth to utter blasphemies against God, blaspheming his name and his dwelling, that is, those who dwell in heaven. Also it was allowed to make war on the saints and to conquer them. And authority was given it over every tribe and people and language and nation, and all who dwell on earth will worship it, everyone whose name has not been written before the foundation of the world in the book of life of the Lamb who was slain. If anyone has an ear, let him hear:

If anyone is to be taken captive,
  to captivity he goes;
if anyone is to be slain with the sword,
  with the sword must he be slain.
Here is a call for the endurance and faith of the saints.

We can see that the Beast will make war with the saints, and the saints are exhorted to be faithful in the midst of their being imprisoned and beheaded.

Revelation 13:15-18

*He was granted power to give breath to the image of the beast, that the image of the beast should both speak and cause as many as would not worship the image of the beast to be killed. He causes all, both small and great, rich and poor, free and slave, to receive a mark on their right hand or on their foreheads, and that **no one may buy or sell except one who has the mark or the name of the beast, or the number of his name**. Here is wisdom. Let him who has understanding calculate the number of the beast, for it is the number of a man: His number is 666.*

So the Beast will kill all who do not worship him. No one will be able to buy or sell unless they have a mark or the name of the Beast or the number of his name (which seems to be 666) on their right hand or forehead. What is clear is that we have the technology to do this right now, although even twenty-five years ago this was considered science fiction.

I want you to consider how long you could go without water, food, shelter, phone, medication, video games, air-conditioning, access to banking and vehicles—all because you refused to take the mark of the Beast. Those who are chipped will have their location known, their conversations recorded, and their every transactions documented. If they happen to help a friend or family member without the mark, they will become an enemy of the Beast. The mark will allow someone to be tortured or killed remotely, depending on what the Beast wants. How long could you go before you would break down? What's the longest you have fasted? How long would you last, especially if you thought you were supposed to be raptured? Would you be embittered toward God? Would you be overwhelmed with despair?

The day of calamity will come in like a flood, and some will say: "God doesn't want me and my family to suffer like this. I'm hungry and thirsty, and I have no meds, and I … I can't go on. Security! Security! Over here! I need water. Yes, okay, I'll worship the Beast. Here's my hand."

You need to understand the clear consequences of taking the mark before calamity comes because, at that point, it will be difficult to make a rational decision. You do know the consequences (even for the elect) of taking the mark, don't you?

Revelation 14:9-12, NLT

Then a third angel followed them, shouting, "Anyone who worships the beast and his statue or who accepts his mark on the forehead or on the hand must drink the wine of God's anger. It has been poured full strength into God's cup of wrath. And they will be tormented with fire and burning sulfur in the presence of the holy angels and the Lamb. The smoke of their torment will rise forever and ever, and they will have no relief day or night, for they have worshiped the beast and his statue and have accepted the mark of his name." This means that God's holy people must endure persecution patiently, obeying his commands and maintaining their faith in Jesus.

This proclamation by the angel clearly delineates to the saints what will be the severe consequence for those who take the mark of the Beast. It is clear that saints will be present during these times of tribulation.

We are about to enter into a season that will require the Body of Christ to be spiritually mature. It's easy being a Christian when there is no cost, no suffering and no lack. The pre-tribulation-rapture doctrine is based on wishful thinking and is leading the people of God to be unprepared for the battle ahead.

Many fill churches and are told that God only wants peace and prosperity for them, but what will happen to their faith when persecution comes? Persecution comes to the Body because we **are** God's people. Since the death of Christ, there have been millions of martyrs who have laid down their lives for the truth. Where can pre-tribbers find justification for not experiencing suffering in the last days, when God's Word states so clearly that we will experience trials and tribulations?

Matthew 16:21-23

From that time Jesus began to show to His disciples that He must go to Jerusalem, and suffer many things from the elders and chief priests and scribes, and be killed, and be raised the third day.
Then Peter took Him aside and began to rebuke Him, saying, "Far be it from You, Lord; this shall not happen to You!"
But He turned and said to Peter, "Get behind Me, Satan! You are an offense to Me, for you are not mindful of the things of God, but the things of men."

The sternest rebuke given to a disciple came from Jesus' reaction to Peter when he tried to tell Jesus that he would not suffer and be killed. What seemed to be an innocent concern for the Master was actually a wicked temptation from the enemy to preserve one's life. This is logical thinking to the carnal man:

Mark 8:35

For whoever desires to save his life will lose it, but whoever loses his life for My sake and the gospel's will save it.

Matthew 10:22-24

And you will be hated by all for My name's sake. But he who endures to the end will be saved. When they persecute you in this city, flee to another. For assuredly, I say to you, you will not have gone through the cities of Israel before the Son of Man comes. A disciple is not above his teacher, nor a servant above his master.

Ephesians 6:11-13

*Put on the whole armor of God, that you may be able to stand against the wiles of the devil. For we do not wrestle against flesh and blood, but against principalities, against powers, against the rulers of the darkness of this age, against spiritual hosts of wickedness in the heavenly places. Therefore take up the whole armor of God, that you may be **able to withstand in the evil day**, and having done all, to stand.*

We wrestle not against men but against principalities, powers, rulers of darkness and spiritual hosts of wickedness.

2 Corinthians 10:4

For the weapons of our warfare are not carnal but mighty in God for pulling down strongholds.

Armor is at our disposal, as believers, but we need to put it on. It will protect us from fear, worry and every accusation. It will allow us to advance and be bearers of light rather than shrinking back into darkness. These weapons are what bring us strength. The enemy will distract many to buy guns and bullets, and these will be useless in the spiritual battle we will need to fight. Many will make plans to save their life by storing food and building secluded protection, yet what will the response be to our neighbors who are perishing? Will we shoot them if they come on our property? How will we share the Gospel from our bunkers?

Although making preparations is prudent, we must look at whether it is just a way to save self. How will we live when our bullets run out and our storehouses are stripped by thieves? I believe that there will be opportunities for us to see great signs and wonders, such as manna from Heaven, water from the rock and our enemies perishing as we worship etc., but we must be in the Spirit and not consumed with fear and trying to save our lives.

The prison doors were opened to Paul and Silas when they were *"praying and singing hymns to God, and the prisoners were listening to them"* (Acts 16:25). They did not run away but, rather, ministered to the prison guard who was about to kill himself for failing to keep charge over his prisoners. They led that man and his family to salvation and baptized them that very night. We see no accounts of Rambo prison raids with guns blazing in the book of Acts. Make no mistake; although the world often see believers as wimps, it is required of us to walk in courage and love.

Today we see a violent offense against traditional Christian values. There is a very purposeful promotion of sexual immorality and perversion onto our culture. The LGBTQ agenda is now being promoted to our children through our public schools and the media and entertainment industries. Anyone who would disagree with these views is labeled as a hater and a bigot. We are in a position where we can no longer ignore how this is gravely affecting the lives of many, especially our children.

In this day and age, there is a cost for declaring your moral beliefs. This can include being banned from social media sites, having your business sued or being fired from your job. These repercussions can happen, not because one is threatening someone or hating someone, but because they are perceived as being threatening.

The Scriptures say that in the last days, good will be considered evil and evil good. It is not the time for the people of God to cower and fear under the powers and principalities of this world. We should not be surprised by these attacks. We must know what we believe. Believers who are homosexuals will be subject to Hell (*Gehenna*) fire, and they will certainly be joined by believers who hate homosexuals. We should note that unbelievers who are living in various forms of sexual immorality are not going to the Lake of Fire for their specific sins, as bad as they are, They, along with unbelievers who may seem to be upstanding citizens, will be judged by whether their sins are atoned for by the blood of Christ. We need to remember that unbelievers are doing what they are supposed to do in their unredeemed state. Our intent is not to win arguments but to save the souls of men who are perishing. These spiritual battles have been going on since the beginning of time, but we should be ready for things to get much worse.

How can we be ready? Jesus said:

Matthew 5:43-48

"You have heard that it was said, 'You shall love your neighbor and hate your enemy.' But I say to you, love your enemies, bless those who curse you, do good to those who hate you, and pray for those who spitefully use you and persecute you, that you may be sons of your Father in heaven; for He makes His sun rise on the evil and on the good, and sends rain on the just and on the unjust. For if you love those who love you, what reward have you? Do not even the tax collectors do the same? And if you greet your brethren only, what do you do more than others? Do not even the tax collectors do so? Therefore you shall be perfect, just as your Father in heaven is perfect."

Eleven of the apostles were martyred for their faith, and John was boiled in oil (even though it did not kill him). He was then sent to a remote and barren island to die of old age. The death of the apostles was not caused by them not fighting hard enough nor not running fast enough; they spoke the truth in love and were not afraid to die, for they knew where they were going. They understood the Gospel of the Kingdom, that if they denied Christ before men, Christ would deny them before His Father. They understood that their Kingdom was to come and that they would do all within their power to share the Gospel with a world that was perishing.

Revelation 12:11

And they overcame him by the blood of the Lamb and by the word of their testimony, and they did not love their lives to the death.

Be ready!

CHAPTER 25

THE PARABLE OF THE SOWER

Matthew 13:18-23

*Therefore hear the parable of the sower: When anyone hears the **word of the kingdom**, and does not understand it, then the wicked one comes and snatches away what was sown in his heart. This is he who received seed by the wayside.*

*But he who received the **seed** [of the kingdom] on stony places, this is he who hears the word and immediately receives it with joy; yet he has no root in himself but endures only for a while. For when tribulation or persecution arises because of the **word** [of the kingdom], immediately he stumbles.*

*Now he who received **seed** [of the kingdom] among the thorns is he who hears the word, and the cares of this world and the deceitfulness of riches choke the **word** [of the kingdom], and he becomes unfruitful.*

*But he who received **seed** [of the kingdom] on the good ground is he who hears the **word** [of the kingdom] and understands it, who indeed bears fruit and produces: some a hundredfold, some sixty, some thirty.*

It is not by chance that the Parable of the Sower in the book of Matthew states that the seed is "**the word of the kingdom.**" The parables that follow this begin with *"the Kingdom of Heaven is like"* and outline the *"gospel of the kingdom."* It is noteworthy that the Parable of the Sower in the book of Luke states that *"the seed is the word of God."*

204

Romans 10:17

*So then faith comes by hearing, and hearing by the **word of God.***

The parable in Luke outlines the "Gospel of grace." Be that as it may, let's look at what happens to the seed, which is *"the word of the kingdom"*:

1. There are some who hear about the Kingdom and don't understand it. The enemy snatches it from their heart. This is the seed that falls by the wayside.

2. There are some who hear the ***"word of the kingdom,"*** understand it and receive it with joy, but then *"when tribulation or persecution arises because of the **word**, immediately he stumbles."* This is like a seed that falls on the stony ground, which has little earth and no root. When the sun rises, the plant is scorched and withers. The scorching sun is the tribulation and persecution that arises when you talk about the *"**word of the Kingdom**."* Understand that this Word will be rejected by the Pharisaical church structure, which is threatened by it. If you try to share this word without having it established in you, you will wither under opposition, and the Word of the Kingdom in you will not go forth.

3. The next ***seed*** (of the Kingdom) takes root, but it falls among thorns, which choke it out. The cares of this world and the deceitfulness of riches are what choke this plant. You might picture this thin, scraggly plant trying to stretch up for sunlight in the midst of these thorns, but they are strangling the life out of it. The plant cannot bear fruit since it is taking all its resources just to survive. Therefore, the plant cannot reproduce because the seeds are in the fruit. So it is with those who are entangled with the cares of this world and the deceitfulness of

riches. The *"word of the kingdom"* will not go forth from them. Instead, many will be wrapped up in their own selfish pursuits. Work, overtime, debt, vacations, entertainment, cars, phones, sports, boats, houses, computers, filling garages, Facebook, restaurants, cat videos, the lusts of the world ... and one barely has time for church. Thorns quickly seek to take over, but how much ground they take is dependent upon how much we let them take. Make no mistake: the righteous will be held to account for what they have produced with the talents they were given.

4. The next seed falls on good soil, this one *"hears the word* [of the kingdom] *and understands it, who indeed bears fruit and produces: some a hundredfold, some sixty, some thirty."* The good soil receives the seed; it germinates, grows up and then produces fruit. Then the seeds of that fruit produce 30, 60 or even 100 other plants of the same variety. The message of the Kingdom is preached, understood and shared. God is calling us to press forward in declaring what He has spoken—even when others don't know what we're talking about or flatly reject it. Is speaking the *"word of the kingdom"* worthwhile? How many of our friends and family members will miss the Kingdom because no one has told them? I venture to say that many will miss it.

The Parable of the Sower starts like this: *"Then He spoke many things to them in parables, saying: 'Behold, a sower went out to sow' "* (Matthew 13:3). I am a sower, and I have just tossed a seed to you. I'm not trying to insinuate that everything that I have said is perfect, but the seed has the fullness of *"the word of the kingdom."* When we press in to understand the mystery of the Kingdom and it begins to make sense and is confirmed by other scriptures and is reflective of whom Jesus said He is, then the mystery transforms into revelation. Whether this seed germinates or grows is not up to me. I've just tossed it out there. Your soil must be prepared, tilled, and have the weeds and thorns taken out, and this plant must be watered and cultivated until there is a harvest which produces seed that can be planted for the next harvest. The Father is glorified when we bear much fruit.

The Parable of the Sower will give you insight into what kind of soil you are. You will be able to look back months from now and see what is produced from the seed that was planted. Will you even remember it? Will you have enough strength to share with those who will otherwise miss the Kingdom? Will you call brothers and sisters to pursue holiness without legalism, so that they might inherit all the promises of God?

CHAPTER 26

SO, WHAT NOW?

If you are like me, you have been greatly challenged by this new Kingdom perspective. I commend you for getting this far. The Gospel of the Kingdom reveals a theological framework of why we must walk in holiness and the consequences if we don't.

I know that not all I have written is perfect. Some of it is conjecture and suggestions as to how things might pan out, but I have presented simple yet profound truths that are meant for us today. I know that there are even more revelations in the Body which will add to and shape what is here. I pray that we test all things with the Word of God.

The present state of the institutional church is diminishing in its power and influence in the world. We need a change, and that doesn't mean the church needs to move faster in what they are presently doing. We have entered into an end-time season that will require the Body of Christ to become spiritually mature. If not, it will be overrun.

The increase in carnality in our culture seems to be increasing exponentially, and so it is also within the Church. There are few leaders who stand firm against the sexual immorality and perversion that engulfs us. Many are willing to tolerate and accept all kinds of perversions for fear of being labeled judgmental or narrow minded. The divorce rate within the church is becoming equal to that of the world. Fear and anxiety, rage and reliance upon medications are soaring. Many look to the Prosperity Gospel to get them out of the financial mess they are currently in. The church's lack of power has been compensated for with new sound and lighting systems and marketing techniques that rival timeshare condos. Now, however, few modern-day Christians have any understanding of why they should fear the Lord, and even fewer are confident of their salvation.

When we repent, we are acknowledging that our sin matters to God. In the process, we must die to our flesh and be cleansed by God's Spirit. This is the process of sanctification. This is the way we are perfected in Christ until He comes. We are confident of who we are in Him because our spirit bears witness that we have opened our hearts and received His wonderful mercy. Yes, it is all "under the blood" ... if we put it under the blood when we repent. This is not only our duty but our great privilege.

We will find that there will be a great outpouring of deliverance and healing as we humble ourselves before the Lord. We will experience the holiness of the Lord like we have never seen, as we seek Him with reverence and rejoice in His goodness toward us.

There are Pharisees and Sadducees today, just as there were in Jesus' day. The Pharisees of His day made all the proper blood sacrifices for the atonement of their sins. They knew and kept the Law and were secure in their heritage. They were confident in their righteousness and rejected any idea that they could be subject to any punishment for carnality. Similarly, there are some today who think they are God's chosen and take no heed to the warnings of Jesus. Jesus was killed by those who thought themselves righteous, those who were angry when confronted with their own unrighteousness. And Jesus warned us that we would be treated in the same way by the Pharisees of our day.

Pharisees and Sadducees are usually well educated, religious and well to do. Many of them are leaders—pastors and priests. Pharisees put themselves on a pedestal, which is where they like to be. They adhere to a strict hierarchal church structure in which they are at the top of the pyramid. They wield power, and they control the money for the lowly laity. The mission of the modern Pharisees is not to equip their members and bring them into maturity but, rather, to expand the size of the pyramid they themselves rule. They control people with rules and regulations and have little interest in those outside their fold.

We see in the following scripture that Pharisees can get converts, but those converts who are discipled by them are ill prepared to stand pure before the Judgment Seat and, therefore, will be twice as likely to end up in Hell (*Gehenna*):

Matthew 23:15

Woe to you, scribes and Pharisees, hypocrites! For you travel land and sea to win one proselyte, and when he is won, you make him twice as much a son of hell [Gehenna] *as yourselves.*

Pharisees look good on the outside, but Christ will be judging their hearts. Those found to be murders, adulterers, having unforgiveness etc. shall not enter into the Kingdom. Not only will Pharisees not enter the Kingdom of Heaven; they will actually prevent other believers from entering:

Matthew 23:13

But woe to you, scribes and Pharisees, hypocrites! For you shut up the kingdom of heaven against men; for you neither go in yourselves, nor do you allow those who are entering to go in.

Luke 11:52

*Woe to you lawyers! For you have taken away the **key of knowledge**. You did not enter in yourselves, and those who were entering in you hindered.*

With some Pharisees, their solemn sacraments performed in ornate hats and robes are required for those who want assurance of eternal security. You wouldn't want to be left out, would you? Some will entice people into a church system which offers those who faithfully attend and tithe an affirmation of their heavenly inheritance without requiring any intimacy with Christ. Some encourage people that they should focus on the gifts of prophecy, casting out of demons and doing signs and wonders, while disregarding the condition of their inner man. You can see that there are a myriad of ways, some subtle and some not so subtle, that a Pharisee can prevent others from entering the Kingdom.

Pharisees and Sadducees become the judges of what constitutes the right standard within their domains. The Sadducees may seem full of mercy and grace, when they tell their people that homosexuality and abortion is acceptable. They will say that God loves you just the way you are. Yet unrepented sin will lead their people into Hell (*Gehenna*). They are the ones who say, "Peace, peace," when there is no peace.

How many sermons have you heard preached about being ready for the Judgment Seat of Christ? How many are seduced into putting their trust in what man says more than in what the Word of God says? True believers would not let any unforgiveness or bitterness have a place in them, and they would not treat pornography like it was some kind of harmless video game. The Scriptures say, *"Flee sexual immorality"* (1 Corinthians 6:18), but the Sadducees rebuke any call to holiness as legalism.

Matthew 23:33-34

Serpents, brood of vipers! How can you escape the condemnation of Hell? Therefore, indeed, I send you prophets, wise men, and scribes: some of them you will kill and crucify, and some of them you will scourge in your synagogues and persecute from city to city,

211

Why is it that the Pharisees want to kill the prophets? The prophets bring warning to the people of God that if they continue in their sin they will receive a harsh judgment. These warnings from God reveal that He desires to grant mercy rather than judgment, and this is the heart of God. The Gospel of the Kingdom that Jesus preached to the righteous was a warning to be ready for the Judgment Seat so as not to miss the Kingdom and suffer punishment. Why have the Pharisees throughout time been enraged by these simple prophetic proclamations? Aren't these prophetic words life for those who hear them?

Pharisees are threatened when prophets speak because they lose control and are no longer the spokesperson for God. They would rather accuse the prophets before the laity and maintain control than for their people to hear the Lord and live. They want to be intermediaries between God and man, and they want to be paid well for their services. Pharisees still take money as a "seed offering," which is required from anyone who wants to receive a prosperity anointing from the rich man of God. No matter how many Bible verses are used by these charlatans, they minister to the carnal man and not the spiritual man. This corruption will be exposed at the Judgment Seat for what it is.

The *"word of the kingdom"* is contrary to many mainline seminary teachings. How many pastors will risk their position and pensions to warn those who will suffer judgment if this word is contrary to their denomination's teaching? I pray that many will sell all they have to acquire the Pearl of Great Price, which is the Kingdom of Heaven.

John 12:42-43

Nevertheless even among the rulers many believed in Him, but because of the Pharisees they did not confess Him, lest they should be put out of the synagogue; for they loved the praise of men more than the praise of God.

The church is at a crossroads right now. In the days to come, we will see many of today's self-proclaimed prophets and apostles being left behind unless they bow in repentance (since many have been leaders in this Pharisaical system). The true prophetic shakes the Pharisee s' church system. Like one who would strike a hornet's nest, expect to be stung in the days ahead.

Not all who disagree with "the Gospel of the Kingdom" are Pharisees, but all Pharisees will disagree with it. Read that again if you need to.

I believe that in the same way that John the Baptist preached repentance in preparation for the coming of Jesus, there will be another mighty call to repentance to prepare for the Second Coming of Jesus. John was in the desert; he was not in the synagogues because he was preaching a different Gospel than the one preached by the scribes and Pharisees.

And so it is today. There is an enormous contingent of faithful men and women who would rather be in the wilderness than enjoy the comforts of a Pharisaical church system. Those who love God are hungering and thirsting for something more than programs, meetings and success. The call to repentance is arising and the Body will walk in holiness, which will cause many to be Kingdom focused, strengthened in community and abounding in fruitfulness.

Matthew 24:14

And this gospel of the kingdom will be preached in all the world as a witness to all the nations, and then the end will come.

I believe this Word will not be delivered by one man, but it will be delivered to the nations by many who see it and believe it, people like you and me. We should be moved by the love of God to share the Gospel of Grace with unbelievers and also to share the Gospel of the Kingdom with believers. My children believe in the Lord, but I want them with me in the Kingdom, and I want my grandkids in the Kingdom too. I want you and yours to be in the Kingdom! I want my enemies to be in the Kingdom! But the message of the Kingdom is hidden and needs to be declared to our brothers and sisters in Christ. Otherwise they will suffer great loss.

Matthew 13:13-16

>   *Therefore I speak to them in parables, because seeing they do not see, and hearing they do not hear, nor do they understand. And in them the prophecy of Isaiah is fulfilled, which says:*
>
>   *"Hearing you will hear and shall not understand,*
>   *And seeing you will see and not perceive;*
>   *For the hearts of this people have grown dull.*
>   *Their ears are hard of hearing,*
>   *And their eyes they have closed,*
>   *Lest they should see with their eyes and hear with their ears,*
>   ***Lest they should understand with their hearts and turn,***
>   ***So that I should heal them****."*
>
>   *But blessed are your eyes for they see, and your ears for they hear.*

Jesus stated that He spoke in parables because the hearts of the people had grown dull, and they barely saw or heard and did not perceive. When we understand the parables, we turn and repent and He can heal us.

This phrase *"heal them"* is also translated as "to make them whole and free from sin." If people understood the Parable of the Unforgiving Servant, they would know how God will judge their unforgiveness, and they would turn from unforgiveness and be made whole. Those who do not see or hear will suffer for it.

How will we stand in this age against the flood of temptations without the fear of the Lord? If I know I can lose the inheritance of the Kingdom if I get caught up with pornography, this gives me the resolve to say, "NO!" I will not lose my inheritance for a bowl of soup!

Job 28:28

And to man He said,
"Behold, the fear of the LORD, that is wisdom,
And to depart from evil is understanding."

Acts 9:31

Then the churches throughout all Judea, Galilee, and Samaria had peace and were edified. And walking in the fear of the Lord and in the comfort of the Holy Spirit, they were multiplied.

A substantial part of the gospels are made up of the parables, the interpretation of the parables, about the Kingdom, about Hell and about repentance. If most of the church doesn't understand these things, then the Gospel has been watered down. The disciples needed all these words for the task that was before them, as we do today!

Matthew 9:35

Then Jesus went about all the cities and villages, teaching in their synagogues, preaching the gospel of the kingdom, and healing every sickness and every disease among the people.

The revelation of the Word of the Kingdom will cause believers to wholeheartedly give of their resources, talents and life to pursue righteousness with vigor and joy with those of like mind. We will see communities arise that are more than just a once-a-week experience. What would Heaven on Earth be like? The early Church understood the Kingdom, and their community expressed this belief. It affected how they lived and how they died.

Matthew 13:44

> *Again, the kingdom of heaven is like treasure hidden in a field, which a man found and hid; and for joy over it he goes and sells all that he has and buys that field.*

It is time to take the Kingdom.

Visit us at: www.thekingdomofheavenislike.com

Matthew 13:10-11

And the disciples came and said to Him, "Why do You speak to them in parables?"

He answered and said to them, "Because it has been given to you to know the mysteries of the kingdom of heaven, but to them it has not been given."

Jesus then told the disciples the following parables:

The Parable of the Sower
The Parable of the Mustard Seed
The Parable of the Leaven
The Parable of the Treasure in the Field
The Parable of the Pearl of Great Price

Jesus ended His teachings with this:

Matthew 13:51-53

Jesus said to them, "Have you understood all these things?"
*They said to Him, **"Yes, Lord."***
Then He said to them, "Therefore every scribe instructed concerning the kingdom of heaven is like a householder who brings out of his treasure things new and old."
Now it came to pass, when Jesus had finished these parables, that He departed from there.

Author Contact Page

You can contact the author in the following ways:

Tom McManus
700 Heatherly Heights Road
Saluda, NC, 28773

tom@thekohislike.com

www.thekohislike.com
www.thekingdomofheavenislike.com

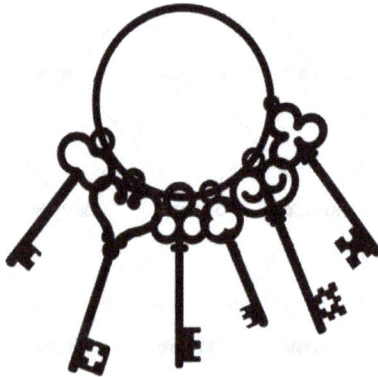

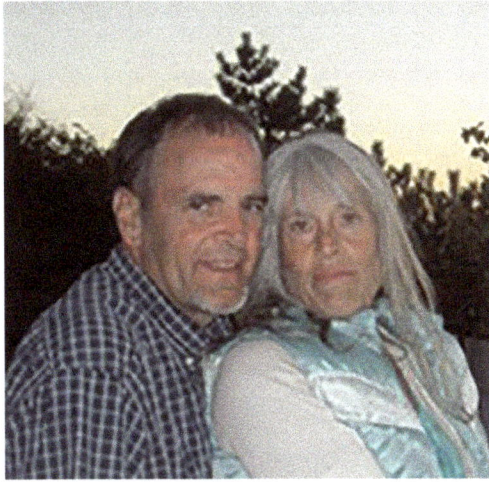

Tom McManus is passionate in calling the Body of Christ to be ready for the Lord's coming. Today many would desire to hear words of comfort and prosperity rather than a call to holiness through repentance. Tom has delved into the Scriptures to unlock what will happen to believers who are carnal and unprepared. When we understand God's judgments we can stand with confidence and full assurance and be ready for His coming.

Tom was born and raised in Boston, Massachusetts, and, although he has been in North Carolina for more than twenty years now, folks still ask him where he's really from.

Parents of three and grandparents of eight, Tom and his wife, Janie, live in the hills of Saluda, North Carolina.

www.ingramcontent.com/pod-product-compliance
Lightning Source LLC
Chambersburg PA
CBHW051208090426
42740CB00021B/3421